DELETE

THE

ADJECTIVE

Sloane,

    The sky is the limit. Your adjectives describe you; never let them define you.

RLTW!

[signature]

DELETE THE ADJECTIVE

A ~~MARRIED~~ ~~WHITE~~ ~~FEMALE~~ ~~ATYPICAL~~ MOTHER ~~MIDDLE-AGED~~ SOLDIER'S ADVENTURES IN RANGER SCHOOL

LISA JASTER

DISCLAIMER

The views expressed in this publication are those of the author and do not necessarily reflect the official policy or position of the Department of Defense or the US government.

Most of the names of fellow Ranger Students and Ranger Instructors have been changed in order to minimize any impact on them or their careers, good or bad.

HOUNDSTOOTH
PRESS

Delete the Adjective
A Soldier's Adventures in Ranger School

ISBN 978-1-5445-3644-6 Hardcover
      978-1-5445-3643-9 Paperback
      978-1-5445-3642-2 Ebook
      978-1-5445-3645-3 Audiobook

To all those who tried and failed—
your "place shall never be with those cold and timid souls
who neither know victory nor defeat."

—THEODORE ROOSEVELT

CONTENTS

INTRODUCTION

*"It is not the critic who counts; not the man
who points out how the strong man stumbles, or where
the doer of deeds could have done them better.
The credit belongs to the man who is actually in the arena,
whose face is marred by dust and sweat and blood;
who strives valiantly; who errs, who comes short again
and again, because there is no effort without error and
shortcoming; but who does actually strive to do the deeds;
who knows the great enthusiasms, the great devotions;
who spends himself in a worthy cause;
who at the best knows in the end the triumph of
high achievement, and who at the worst, if he fails,
at least fails while daring greatly, so that his place
shall never be with those cold and timid souls
who neither know victory nor defeat."*

—THEODORE ROOSEVELT, "Citizenship in a Republic"
(popularly known as "The Man in the Arena")

My squad and I were given our assignment. We conducted a recon, and I straight-up stalked to ten feet from the enemy objective, moving first in a hunched walk, then crawling, and then pulling myself along on my elbows with my belly low to the ground. The ground was covered in small bushes and prickly shrubs, and the Georgia clay was both unforgiving and slick in the humid spring months. Low crawling through this slimy maze of undergrowth was no small feat because I had a bunch of strings hanging off my body. Ranger School made you dummy cord every piece of gear to yourself so you couldn't lose anything. That was a great supply policy, but it sucked to move through brush while all your mandated strings snag on every bush.

The men pretending to be Opposition Forces (OP4) had no idea I was lurking in the woods, just out of arm's reach.

I was only discovered because our instructor—also known as the Ranger Instructor (RI)—pointed me out to them. At that point, I had to "fight" in place rather than retreat. I couldn't escape because I was now knotted up with the local flora. We had a brief shootout using blanks, and I "died."

I thought I did amazing because I got so close to my targets. Then the RI reminded me I was conducting reconnaissance, not hunting. My goal wasn't to neutralize the objective but rather collect intel for higher headquarters to support follow-on missions and avoid getting compromised.

After the RI reamed me for my failure to complete the mission, I thanked him. He didn't know how to react to the fact that I thanked him for his feedback, enjoyed the education, and felt invigorated by the experience. That wasn't the usual reaction he got. But honestly, I had learned a lot and enjoyed myself. I just felt honored to be able to be a part of the school and in the field with these future leaders.

I was covered in scrapes and bug bites, the skin was peeling off my feet, and I had never smelled worse in my entire life. And I was having a blast. This was where I was meant to be.

MILITARY HISTORY

As a child, my exposure to the military included the recruiter at the mall—Sergeant First Class (SFC) Newby is a friend to this day —and the guys who marched in the Memorial Day parade carrying the American flag. But my biggest influence in terms of my military career was my dad. My dad graduated from West Point in 1968 branching Armor and shortly thereafter attended Ranger School. He completed three tours in Vietnam, receiving four Purple Hearts and a Silver Star for bravery. The Silver Star is the third-most prestigious military award for valor.[1] By the time I was born, he was 90 percent medically retired from the military and retained only loose ties with West Point, except when Army played Navy in football.

I followed in my dad's footsteps, attending Cadet Basic Training through graduation at West Point (1996–2000). While there, I

---

[1] "Silver Star Medal and Ribbon," Military Medals, accessed September 12, 2022, http://www.militarymedals.com/medals/silver-star-medal/.

earned my Bachelor of Science degree in civil engineering. I served in the US Army on active duty from graduation until February 2007, when I chose to explore options outside the military. I left active duty for a plethora of reasons, including the needs of my new marriage and the promise of stability. My husband was a Marine captain and had recently transitioned from active duty to reserve; to make a long story short, the life I could have outside the military with him looked a lot better than the life an active-duty career would afford us.

However, I never found a "tribe" in corporate America like the one I cherished during my time in uniform, so in 2012, I joined the reserve. At the time, I had a fantastic job at Shell Oil Company and loved my coworkers, but it ended at the office. Shell was a career, but the military was a lifestyle, and I wanted that version of me back.

Then, in 2015, at the age of thirty-seven, I had the opportunity to attend Ranger School. This was something I had never even considered during my active-duty days. That door was closed to women, and I wasn't knocking on it. But suddenly, the door opened a crack, and I couldn't help but push my way through.

I have spent my life on a trajectory of self-improvement for a variety of reasons, some selfish and some altruistic. Every time I reach a set goal, I set my sights on the next mountain to climb. There are a couple goals I don't think I will ever reach, but I will kill myself trying. First and foremost, I want to be a fantastic mother, wife, and Christian. I know I will never reach the end of that journey and I fail much more often than I succeed. My second, and longest-running, goal is to be the type of person who can positively lead through hard times. I can only do this if people are willing to follow me and I can be levelheaded and rational during stressful situations. In the military, one of the best tests of a person's ability to lead through adversity is Ranger School.

As a soldier, I wanted to be as well trained as possible. As an engineer, I wanted to know how to best support the tip of the spear, understanding what our combat soldiers require to best execute their mission. As a leader, I needed to be well tested and ready for whatever situation the military might throw at me. Attending Ranger School would allow me to achieve all of these objectives—and when I got there, I found I was a round peg in a round hole.

WHAT IS RANGER SCHOOL?

Ranger School is among the Army's toughest schools. It's a premier small-unit tactics and leadership school that develops skills for engaging the enemy in close combat. The school isn't as much of a training opportunity as it is a testing opportunity. Infantry officers and non-commissioned officers (NCOs) who want to reach their highest potential need to prove their grit by earning the coveted Ranger Tab. Additionally, anyone who wants to remain in the elite Ranger Regiment must attend and pass Ranger School. Three Ranger battalions oversee training at the school. They are all battle-tested, tabbed Rangers. Many of the cadre and support staff have deployed multiple times with the Ranger Regiment to places like Iraq, Afghanistan, Djibouti, and various other locations. Some have not spent time in deployable Ranger units but excelled in their previous military positions. They are all the best at what they do.

There are three phases to the course (Darby, Mountains, and Swamps), which test students in a range of environments. The grueling nature of Ranger School can be summed up by the numbers. If you go straight through without having to repeat any of the parts, it is sixty-one days long. During the course, students carry rucks that weigh between sixty and ninety pounds and walk over two hundred miles while averaging 2,200 calories and four and a half hours of sleep a day.

Historical graduation rates hover around 50 percent on average.[2] To get to the finish line, a student must:

- Pass all events during Ranger Assessment Phase (RAP) week
- Average more than 50 percent "Go"s on graded patrols, meaning they have to do well when assigned a leadership position on the tested small-unit tactics
- Score well on peer evaluations; in other words, their fellow squad mates don't think they suck
- Act right with a focus on safely executing the mission
- Stay healthy

In most cases, if you fail in one of these areas, you get "recycled." Many people—about 34 percent of those who ultimately

---

[2] Airborne and Ranger Training Brigade, "ARTB Command Brief," Fort Benning: U.S. Army Fort Benning and The Maneuver Center of Excellence, May 4, 2021, https://www.benning.army.mil/Infantry/ARTB/Student-Information/content/PDF/Ranger%20School%20web11.pdf?04MAY2021.

graduate—recycle, or repeat, one or more phases of the school.[3] That means they have to start Darby, Mountains, or Swamps over from the beginning. Sometimes, students are recycled back to the very beginning of Ranger School, or Day One. God help you if you are a Day One recycle because you will need faith and grit to survive that kick in the gut.

Unless you have experience with Ranger School, you might not know what a "normal" experience leading up to it looks like. A typical Ranger School candidate is twenty-three years old, usually active duty, and spends months preparing to attend. Most candidates are combat arms, specifically infantry, but every support branch needs to fill a quota of Ranger Qualified Soldiers to support the Ranger Regiment. Preparation may be as little as doing harder physical training (PT) each morning with a group that wants to go to the school, or as advanced as learning the tactics tested at Ranger School, going over battle drills, and running mock missions. Less than 1 percent of the Army is Ranger qualified. Very few National Guard soldiers attend, and even fewer reservists get one of the coveted slots because there is only one infantry unit in the US Army Reserve.

My experience at Ranger School wasn't "normal," and neither was my preparation. There was no Ranger School-preparation platoon I could sign up for, no special-unit PT sessions, and no Ranger mentorship program that allowed women to join. Hell, there wasn't even a "female" option on the Ranger School Physical Exam form.

---

3   Michelle Tan, "Ranger School: Many Do-Overs Rare, Not Unprecedented," Army Times, September 18, 2015, https://www.armytimes.com/news/your-army/2015/09/18/ranger-school-many-do-overs-rare-not-unprecedented/.

The one thing that really was normal about my experience was that I wrote everything in a little, green notebook we all HAD to keep in our pockets. Most of my fellow students wrote out lists of foods they were going to eat, movies they wanted to see, or other things they were looking forward to doing when they got home. My scribblings were more focused on making sure I could someday explain my absence to my little ones. I kept a lot of notes in Ranger School. I wrote letters to family and friends. To stay awake in the patrol base, I wrote down my thoughts, the mission information for the day, the food I was craving, and anything else going through my mind. Everyone filled a few tactical notebooks because each day started with an order and mission information. To remember grid coordinates, passwords, and leadership information, an exhausted person takes copious notes. I came home with a couple little, green notebooks and had written letters to my family almost every day. There wasn't much to discuss in those letters, and I wasn't receiving mail regularly, so I sent my family anything that came to mind, including statistics, meals, and stories of squad mates. I referenced all those letters and notebooks to build the following story.

DELETE THE ADJECTIVE

Gayle Tzemach Lemmon describes the women she interviewed for her book *Ashley's War* as wanting to "live in the **and**." That phraseology perfectly reflects how I felt. I wanted to be feminine **and** badass. I didn't want one to limit the other.

When I finally had the opportunity to attempt Ranger School, fifteen years after my male peers, I realized the barrier to believing specific people can succeed in a certain culture, world, or activity was based only on individual experiences. Many of the men I encountered referenced the ladies in their lives when trying to rationalize why I wouldn't want to shave my head and sleep in the woods. Unless one of these alpha males knew someone like me, it was impossible for them to comprehend that the adjectives they saw only painted a fraction of the picture. They missed everything after the *and*. If I completed the course as both a woman and a reservist, I would demonstrate that tactical and technical capabilities lie in unexpected and untapped places within our armed forces. My Ranger School aspirations were never about fighting for social causes. But I do want people to understand that adjectives are descriptors, not limiters.

I may have been a different type of Ranger student, but I was made for that school.

I share my experience now to make it clear that my adjectives —female, old, reserve—don't define me. For my six months at Ranger School, I was simply another Ranger student who underwent all the same tests my classmates did—and then some. Of course, the other students weren't competing with desk jockeys at *People Magazine* and other noncredible sources proclaiming I received extra food and took more showers than the male students. For me, going to Ranger School was the right way to prove to both supporters and doubters that merit should always trump adjectives. Wanting to be the best at your chosen profession and pushing through obstacles to get there should be the norm, not the outlier.

My story shows that adjectives aren't destiny. If you are a doubter or a skeptic, this book is for you. If you think you can't break out of your own little box of adjectives, this book is for you.

One of my favorite things to say now is, "Adversity doesn't build character, it reveals it." I am sure I am not the first person to put those words together. Whoever did was so very right. When a person fails or succeeds, I am not interested in their adjectives, I am interested in their reactions. When you fail your patrol, can you suck it up and help your buddy pass? Better yet, after you pass your patrol, can you reach down and help lift up those who are struggling to succeed? When the mountains are high and the packs are heavy, can you smile at a beautiful sunset and share a moment of serenity with your battle buddy?

This is the story of my reactions as I stretched myself to the limits and lived fully in the *and*.

CHAPTER 1

STEPPING INTO
THE ARENA

"Recognizing that I volunteered as a Ranger,
fully knowing the hazards of my chosen profession,
I will always endeavor to uphold the prestige, honor,
and high esprit de corps of the Rangers.

"Acknowledging the fact that a Ranger is a more elite soldier
who arrives at the cutting edge of battle by land, sea,
or air, I accept the fact that as a Ranger my country
expects me to move further, faster, and fight
harder than any other soldier.

"Never shall I fail my comrades[.] I will always keep
myself mentally alert, physically strong, and morally straight,
and I will shoulder more than my share of the task whatever
it may be, one hundred percent and then some.

"Gallantly will I show the world that I am a specially selected and well-trained soldier. My courtesy to superior officers, neatness of dress, and care of equipment shall set the example for others to follow.

"Energetically will I meet the enemies of my country. I shall defeat them on the field of battle, for I am better trained and will fight with all my might. Surrender is not a Ranger word. I will never leave a fallen comrade to fall into the hands of the enemy, and under no circumstances will I ever embarrass my country.

"Readily will I display the intestinal fortitude required to fight on to the Ranger objective and complete the mission, though I be the lone survivor."

—**RANGER CREED**[4]

THE CALM BEFORE THE STORM

On September 9, 2014, I received an email from my military unit's senior NCO, Sergeant Major (SGM) Payne. It simply stated, "Major (MAJ) Jaster, you're being talked about in high places. SGM P." After scrolling through multiple forwards, I saw an overly wordy email written by the 38th Chief of Staff

---

[4]   "Ranger Creed," in Ranger Handbook: Training Circular No. 3-21.76 (Washington, DC: Headquarters, Department of the Army, April 2017).

of the Army, GEN Raymond T. Odierno. These types of general officer monologues got the auto-delete from me because being a mom, wife, reservist, and project manager made allocating time to the Army's latest "theme" impossible. But my sergeant major never wasted my time. Hidden in paragraph three of six was, "The Ranger course assessment would include female soldiers as course students..."

I had to read it several times before the gravity of what SGM Payne was implying hit me. It took me three days to compose my response: "Now that would be something...old and a girl!!!"

I briefly let my mind drift to the school. I knew lots of guys who had earned the coveted Ranger Tab, and I had a pretty solid understanding of the course. But I knew deep down there wasn't a single aspect of my life (mom, wife, project manager, reservist) that was pointing me toward a school like that. Ranger School was a dream for my twenty-year-old self. At thirty-six, about to turn thirty-seven, I was worried about more pressing matters.

That night, I mentioned the email to Allan, my husband. I didn't really know how I expected him to react, but he was immediately and emphatically supportive. His confidence in me came from a place of experience, as he had completed plenty of difficult schools as a marine.

We looked up the standards. I laughed and said there was no way I could make that run. Five miles in forty minutes—forget it! I was in a weird spot where I wasn't ready to let myself believe I would even be considered for that famously difficult school. And I damn sure wasn't ready to discuss what being a "first" might mean. Allan, on the other hand, had zero problem saying, "You were made for this, love. You should do it."

Try as I might, I couldn't get that email out of my mind. My mom had a favorite saying when I was a kid, "Never say you could've, should've, or would've." I felt her nagging presence and wondered how Ranger School would do against her could've/should've/would've scale.

As I thought about my decision, I knew this wasn't just my individual sacrifice to make. My boss, my husband, and especially my children were going to potentially pay a higher cost than I was for this endeavor. Was that fair to them? Would I be stealing precious moments from my family I would later regret giving up? For members of our military, leaving their families for long deployments or training events is common. But those separations are job requirements. They don't typically volunteer to leave their job, family, and supportive husband to seek glory and break barriers. I needed to make sure I was doing it for the right reasons and that those who cared for me most supported it.

After hours of wrestling with the question of whether Ranger School was the right decision for me, I took the plunge. Just weeks before my thirty-seventh birthday, I sent my name and social security number into the Department of the Army via my military chain of command and waited. I had no idea what to expect, what the timeline was going to be, or how the Army was going to choose its guinea pigs. All I knew was if I didn't try, I might regret it forever.

When I announced to my friends and family that I had thrown my name into the ring for Ranger School, Jason, a friend from West

Point, sent me a note. Reading it now, I am still amazed at the strength of the military tribe. I hadn't seen Jason in almost fifteen years, and I had no idea how impactful his words were going to be to me in the upcoming months.

22 October 2014

Lisa,

Decided to pass a note along with the book and tab. The tab. The tab is known as a "Drive On" tab. In the Infantry, your first line supervisor (enlisted mainly) gives you the tab off of their uniform. It is to remind you that it can be done—and others have made it before you. Usually, you put these in your patrol cap (sewn in—or otherwise secured), I carried mine in my left breast pocket (old uniform). Mine came from my dad, so it was pretty important for me. You will also need another tab—go buy one—that goes in another uniform or cap. This one is the one you will put on your uniform after graduation (after the pinning ceremony). One is to show you that what you are doing is not impossible; the other is to remind you of the risks/rewards, or the "why." When you graduate, you give the Drive On tab back to the person you got it from. In older traditions, the person you got the tab from was not allowed to wear theirs again until their subordinate graduated—not failed—but graduated. The point of the second was to highlight that being a Ranger isn't just about graduating a school but to train your subordinates/successors to replace you—as a Ranger should. If your subordinate could not pass Ranger School, then you were unfit to wear your tab as well—so you better get to training that kid. I will not wear my tab when you go to school in support of you going—unless there is a situation where I need to wear it (I'm an ORSA working with IN and need the credibility, etc.).[5]

I have the utmost respect for you for deciding to go—especially at our age. You can do it. Never quit—make them graduate you or kill you, those are the options.

Go hogs!

Jay

Jay's note represented so much more than a friend who had my back. His words proved the time was right to push through the old status quo. If my peers, the guys who had been leading soldiers into combat for fifteen-plus years, could get behind me, then I owed it to them to give this my all. There was absolutely no reason for him to reach out. He had nothing to gain, and we hadn't stayed in touch. This was pure, unadulterated, unsolicited support, and it meant the world to me. That tab stayed with me every step of the way, and when I got back to Houston, I met him, his wife, and his daughter for lunch so I could return it to him.

PREPARING

It was time to test my thirty-seven-year body of work, from building resilience as a kid, to discipline I learned dancing from the ages of three to eighteen, to tactics that flooded my life from 1996 to today, and finally to the fitness I had been building since leaving the Army.

---

[5]   ORSA is Operations Research/Systems Analysis. IN is Infantry.

I stepped up my training regimen. In addition to my regular CrossFit and Jiu Jitsu workouts, I started wearing a weighted vest everywhere I went. I would ruck run to my daughter's daycare and then ruck march back with her sitting on top of my pack. As I trained, I repeated the Ranger Creed to myself until I had it memorized.

Victoria providing additional weight for my training by sitting in my ruck sack.

I also worked on my tactical skills. My husband pulled out the range finder, and when we went for walks, he would bet me push-ups on how far away random objects were from us. Being able to estimate distances quickly and accurately is a critical soldier skill.

Paperwork was going to be a huge hurdle. For example, I had to get a full physical. Since I wasn't stationed at a military base, I didn't have access to a military medical facility, which presented a pretty big challenge. So, on December 23, I brought the "Ranger Physical" paperwork and a blank check to a local Houston walk-in emergency clinic and asked them to help me fill it out. Upon arrival, we discovered a second issue with completing the paperwork. No woman had ever had a Ranger School physical. The paperwork asked doctors to check stuff I just didn't have. Further, it neglected other items that probably needed checking. To add to the fun, I was over thirty-five, which apparently meant near death in Army years. As such, I was subjected to additional poking and prodding, all under the banner of "medical precaution." After four hours and almost $1,000, I had all the tests completed and the forms filled out to the best of my ability. I was certain they were wrong, or something was missing, but I didn't know what right looked like.

Only days before I was supposed to report to the first integrated Ranger Training Assessment Course (RTAC), the official hair standards for female Ranger School hopefuls came out—short length, no more than one inch from the scalp, no less than one-quarter of an inch. I won't lie, I questioned my resolve. Everyone was shocked, and several people in leadership warned us ladies not to cut our hair until the last possible moment because the standard seemed crazy. After the initial shock, it made complete sense. Men had to cut their hair to the shortest allowed army standard: shaved heads. One-quarter inch is the shortest allowed standard for women in Army regulations.

I waited until the night before I flew out to Fort Benning to cut my long, red hair. It wasn't just because losing almost eighteen inches of hair was scary; it was also because I hadn't told most people where I was going or what I was doing. As far as my supervisor at work knew, I was just leaving for my two-week military annual training.

I walked into the beauty salon with a printout of the Army short-hair regulation. The beautician kept trying to talk me out of it. I explained I was going to a military school and didn't have a choice. He never seemed to quite understand that. Explaining I wanted to donate it to "Locks of Love" was a better approach. He divided my hair into four sections and put in very tight rubber bands. The idea was he would cut between my scalp and the band to make the donation process neat and tidy. He lost his nerve. His eyes literally welled up, and he had to walk away while I took the scissors and made four very deliberate snips. My beautician just stood with his hands over his mouth as I chopped away. It was done. Nothing says "I'm all in" like cutting your hair.

It turned out I look AWFUL with short hair. First, I have a nice scar on the back of my scalp where my head introduced itself to my father's tri-barb fishing hook one summer as a kid. Second, I don't have the face for it. Believe me, I fully grasped the idea that every time someone mentioned my short hair, it would be a reminder of Ranger School. That reminder was either going to be a cool story, or it wasn't.

When I got home, Allan tried to make me feel better by pretending to barely notice. He told me, "I married you for your legs. I don't care at all about your hair." My daughter fussed quite a bit, wondering if she would have to cut her hair, too. My son, the bravest of all, told me I was still beautiful on the inside.

PREQUALIFYING

As part of our preparation, all the female soldiers were required to graduate the RTAC. This two-week training was a crash course to make sure we were ready for Ranger School.

I left for RTAC on January 14, 2015. I dropped Zac off at school knowing I would be back in two weeks. We knew the drill from my reserve annual training. Too easy. Then, I walked Tori into daycare. Her teacher asked who I was because I looked so different. I explained to the teacher I would be away for two weeks and have no contact with the kids. The bottom fell out. The gravity of what I was about to do hit me. For just a second, I longed to just go home and cuddle on the couch with my kids, leaving this craziness for someone else. Then I got in my car and changed from Mom to Lisa to MAJ Jaster.

Time to either make history or go home with a shaved head.

I definitely had some successes and failures during RTAC. We took a sample water-survival test in a pool on post. After jumping off the five-meter diving board wearing blacked out goggles, each soldier had to swim to the side of the pool while retaining their gear. My rig slid off over my head as soon as I hit the water. I guess at five-foot-four and 140 pounds, I was slightly smaller than the typical Ranger School hopeful. So I held my gear and rubber rifle over my head, rather than attempting to put it back on, while side stroking to the side of the pool. The RIs broke character at this point and let a few audible, "Holy shit," "She's good," and "That girl can swim" comments slip. For about ten seconds, I remembered I was proving some women can actually add value to a combat environment to an entire group of people, men and women. *Hell, yeah. I got this*, I thought. It felt damn good. Until I smiled with pride, at which point I got to do a few extra flutter kicks on the side of the pool for my lack of military bearing.

Sometime after pool PT, we transitioned to training and testing our ability to navigate through the woods. The word on the street was that the land-navigation (land-nav) course at RTAC was harder than the one at Ranger School. My last actual land-nav experience was in 2005 at Fort Leonard Wood, where the terrain was easy to read due to hills and other land formations. At Benning, not so much. There was a time when I had been a land-nav goddess, but that was many moons ago. I was worried and started the day with a sour feeling in the pit of my belly. I knew people expected me to fail land-nav.

However, my doubts were misplaced. My husband was an avid hunter when I met him, and I fell in love with the sport after we married. A large part of my life was spent in the woods, following tracks or trying to find the truck. Those hunting skills paid dividends at RTAC. Every time I found my point, my confidence grew, and my fatigue melted away. I found all my points and was back to turn in my score sheet before almost everyone else. I didn't look at any of the RIs' faces or smile when the RI said, "Seven out of seven points, Jaster. Go get on your gear." I didn't feel like flutter kicking again.

Another critical point of success or failure was how the other soldiers felt about you. We did Peers at RTAC that mimicked the ones in Ranger School. "Peers" is the military-school equivalent of voting someone off the island in *Survivor*. Every single student rank ordered their squad mates and then answered a couple questions about them. I peered rather well and received excellent feedback during the process. One of the girls who passed everything peered low and started crying. A huge factor in leadership is the ability to deal with stress and still make calm, rational decisions without being so cold you negate the impact of emotions and personalities. There were plenty of guys who reacted badly to their peer results as well, but they weren't trying to be the first. Trying to break barriers adds a significant emotional burden. It was a hard pill to swallow, but you can't cry about not being liked, at least, not in public, and expect to lead soldiers into battle.

HAVING THE TALK

During that first RTAC, the Army introduced the Observer/Advisor (OA) program. I think a bunch of senior combat-arms officers, males from a different generation, made their decisions without involving women like me in the discussion. Based on some of the bizarre requirements imposed on the female students, they may not have consulted any women at all.

I'm sure the women who volunteered to be OAs did so with the greatest intentions, but I still hated the program. Anything different in Ranger School when the women were there automatically undermined the credibility of the integrated course. I get that bras and feminine-hygiene products needed to be added to the packing list, but those were minor changes. Adding these non-Ranger-qualified women only made the RIs feel like their integrity was in question before the course even started. NCOs are expected to be professionals. Individuals attending the Army's premier leadership course are expected to be professionals. I didn't need additional people walking around taking care of my femininity when I went hunting or to the field with my regular unit, so why was it required here? From the outside looking in, the existence of the program told the American public the RIs at Ranger School weren't professional enough to be trusted and needed someone to oversee their behavior.

Of course, any changes to the course impacted how other soldiers saw the female candidates. There was a Ranger candidate named Johnson who constantly made passive-aggressive comments about women attending RTAC. One night, he decided to have an interesting chat with another soldier remarkably close to my bed. It was time to address the elephant in the room.

"Okay, Johnson, spill it," I said, extremely calmly and nonchalantly. "Why don't you think women belong in Ranger School?"

I suspected he was gunning for a fight about it and wouldn't shy away from a little confrontation. I wasn't mad at him. I also guessed his feelings were common. I was one of the first women to sleep in these barracks since the school was founded in 1950. Change is hard for organizations and people, especially in the military.

Johnson was about three years old when I joined the Army in 1996, and he was full of piss and vinegar. I opened the floodgates with my question, and he let all his frustrations with integration flow for quite some time. "You fucking expect some chick to have my back when we are under fire?!"

I quickly backed him off to discuss the issue at hand. "Yeah, I get the infantry thing. But why don't you want women HERE?" He looked stupefied, as if that was what he'd been talking about the entire time, so I explained, "I'm not talking about joining the infantry. I am asking you, after training next to me for the past week, why do you deserve to be here more than I do? The Army brags that Ranger School is the top leadership school in the nation, and I am a leader. Men in support roles regularly get slots, so why shouldn't women? How could I ever reach the same ranks and level of respect as my peers if I wasn't even allowed to attend my service's premier leadership school?"

By the time we had this conversation, we already knew which of the 125 candidates were the weak ones. That list did NOT include me. I needed him to look at me and, while evaluating my performance over the past six days, tell me why I, Lisa Jaster, didn't deserve to be here as much as he did. He, like many others, could only see women as his mom, his sister, his wife, his friends.

I had to remind him that those women weren't me. And I was not them. His limited perspective was based on his very valid experiences, but he hadn't trained with a Lisa Jaster before. His position that women didn't belong had weakened over the past week, and he knew it. I matched him one for one on push-ups, pull-ups, miles run, obstacles completed, classes taken, etc. What more did he need before he knew I belonged here with him?

The conversation never turned hostile, although it often got quite spirited. He never felt attacked, and I never went on the offensive—or defensive, for that matter. I got it. These boys were alphas, and I was trying to enter their territory. This conversation was important. I had to do it right, and I realized quickly I had better have some fair answers to some hard questions ready regarding women in Ranger School.

Toward the end of the two-week RTAC, Johnson was the class leader. Of all people, he chose me as his platoon sergeant. He had been a royal pain in my ass up to this point and was still the mouthpiece for the "women don't belong here" movement among the students.

With a straight face, I asked Johnson, "Why the hell did you pick me as your right-hand man?" Johnson just snorted and said he knew I would get shit done, even if I was a woman. Looks like Johnson got over himself when he needed a good team.

First major Ranger School lesson learned. Organizational change happens one person at a time.

READY FOR RANGER SCHOOL

YOUR SGLI DEDUCTION INCLUDES TRAUMATIC INJURY PROTECTION (TSGLI)
SPOUSE SGLI COVERAGE: $100,000
RECEIVED CERT OF PERF FOR ORD# 500195
**CONGRATULATIONS ON YOUR COMPLETION OF THE
RANGER ASSESSMENT COURSE. GOOD LUCK AT RANGER
SCHOOL. WE ARE PULLING FOR YOU.
PLEASE VERIFY YOUR STATE OF LEGAL RESIDENCE FOR STATE INCOME
TAX PURPOSE. CONTACT YOUR PAYROLL OFFICE TO FILE A NEW DD FORM
2058 TO CHANGE/ESTABLISH THE CORRECT STATE IMMEDIATELY.
-TRICARE DENTAL PROGRAM RATES INCREASE IN JAN 2015. MORE INFO
 AT WWW.METLIFE.COM/TRICARE
-AFFORDABLE CARE ACT TAX REPORTING INFO, SEE WWW.TRICARE.MIL/ACA
-MILITARY SAVES WEEK, 23-28 FEB 2015. SEE WWW.MILITARYSAVES.ORG
-RECEIPT OF VA COMPENSATION AND MILITARY PAY FOR THE SAME PERIOD
 IS PROHIBITED; REPAYMENT OF ONE OF THE PAYMENTS IS REQUIRED.

DFAS Form 702, Jan 02

*Comments included on the bottom of my pay stub
after graduating RTAC*

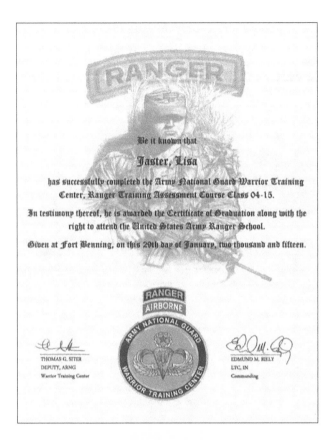

RTAC Diploma

The graduation ceremony at the end of RTAC wasn't all that inspiring, but I was excited to get my diploma. I laughed when I saw my completion certificate still had all male pronouns. The cadre offered to change it when I pointed it out, but I refused. I thought it was perfect just the way it was.

One hundred twenty-five soldiers showed up the first day of RTAC. Fifty-three graduated. I finished second overall. The only thing the guy above me beat me on was push-ups. That was a great way to end the first integrated session. When I read where I placed, I started believing graduation from Ranger School was possible.

CHAPTER 2

QUALIFIED
SOLDIERS

RAP Week

Day 0–Day 5/Week 1/April 18–April 23

Ranger Assessment Phase (RAP) week, the first four days of Ranger School, historically accounts for about 60 percent of the overall failures.[6] During this week, we would be tested on our individual physical fitness and tactics, including swimming, rucking, and navigation abilities. Of the hundred or so women that originally raised their hands for Ranger School, twenty-one made it through RTAC with a cadre recommendation to attend

---

[6] 4th Ranger Training Battalion, "Training Notes: U.S. Army Ranger School: How to Prepare, Avoid Pitfalls," Infantry 101, no. 1 (January–March 2012): 41, https://www .benning.army.mil/infantry/magazine/issues/2012/jan-mar/pdfs/jan-mar12.pdf.

the school. Of that twenty-one, nineteen women showed up for the first-ever integrated Ranger School Class 6-15 (one decided it wasn't for her, and one was injured). Our course was close to the maximum capacity, with 399 people reporting on Day Zero.

RAP week was highly publicized and full of knowns. During RAP week, if you failed an event, you grabbed your gear and got on a plane home. I told myself failing something I could prepare for, physical or administrative, was inexcusable. That was my number one goal: not to get dropped for something I could prepare for.

Now, Day Zero was here, and I was ready. I had never before been this physically prepared for anything. I had my paperwork in order to the best of my ability. I had cut myself off caffeine. I had shaved my head again. And I had said goodbye to my young kids. That was difficult, especially when Zac asked me not to leave, but I have never been the type of parent who just pushes their kids from behind. I will pull, I will push, and I will run next to them. The best thing I could do for my kids was succeed and show them success is about the skills they cultivate, not the adjectives that define them.

ARRIVING AT DARBY

I got a cab to Camp Rogers with two other Ranger hopefuls. It was amusing to watch the other soldiers' faces when the cab pulled up with me already in it. The two young men initially waved off the driver, insisting they were headed to Ranger School and couldn't be delayed by my destination. The cabby happily informed them, "She's going to Ranger School as well!" For a second, the two just stood there, looking at a strange woman eating a Subway sandwich in their ride to Ranger School. Cognitive dissonance at its finest. I just wanted to enjoy my Subway in peace. Seeing no other cabs, the soldiers got in.

I had assumed, quite wrongly, that all the men would know there were going to be women in this Ranger class. Apparently, Ranger School didn't tell them, and not many eighteen- to twenty-two-year-old soldiers read the recent OpEds in the newspapers about us "gals."

I tried to act casual. Once they processed that this middle-aged woman was heading to the same Ranger School they were, the questions flowed—and they had a lot! Their first, and still the hardest to answer, was, "Why the hell would you want to do this?"

Once we arrived, I had to report immediately to the aid station to take a pregnancy test. My cab buddies opted to come with me because they didn't want to leave me alone. I heard one of them say, "Never leave a fallen comrade," straight from the Ranger Creed. I giggled, as I was not dying, I just had to pee in a cup! Of course, the RI laughed at the young men and told them to in-process, but the gesture wasn't lost on me. The RI took notice as well. I wonder if he thought, "Damn, these boys already feel like they need to take care of this lady," or if he saw what really happened. During our fifteen-minute cab ride, two young men had had their world and expectations flipped upside down—and they were completely cool with it.

I successfully in-processed, which meant I passed the first test of Ranger School: getting your paperwork right. Thank GOD!!! This was no small feat, especially considering I completed it with some civilian healthcare workers a few days before Christmas at an urgent care facility.

After finishing our paperwork, the school got locked down for over two hours in the barracks due to a tornado in the vicinity. Our bags stayed outside and were soaked from the storm. Not a great start.

Once the storm passed, we all went out to "the rocks." The rocks was the covered training area at Camp Rogers. It was basically a gravel pit with a freestanding roof above it. We stood by our bags and were divided equally into three companies: Alpha, Bravo, and Charlie. People tried to wargame which company they went to by lining up in certain spots so they could either try to get with their friends or go to the Darby company with the highest pass rate. Thirty minutes into the course, and many were already plotting. Prior to showing up here, I didn't think it mattered at all what training company I was assigned to. Apparently, I was wrong.

I was assigned to Bravo Company (B-Co) and quickly informed B-Co was not good luck for anyone. Apparently, our cadre prided themselves on their Ranger students averaging the least amount of sleep, which can only be gained through additional PT. Perfect. Our company started the course with 134 personnel, including two marines, one airman, seven women, and one foreign officer. I started writing down every statistic I could right then in my pocket notebook because I was a nerd and wanted untainted facts at the end of this experience. I also couldn't remember shit at that point in my life, so I wrote down every name and little quirk people had so I could effectively communicate and efficiently leverage skills as they emerged.

The RIs didn't bother us much on Day Zero. But that didn't mean things were cool, calm, and collected. When dinner rolled around, we had less than ten minutes to eat. The food was so damn hot, I couldn't hold it, and we were only given a spoon—so I grabbed a bunch of napkins and used them like oven mitts. I took one bite and burned the roof of my mouth. In order to get some calories in without causing further physical harm to myself, I poured apple juice onto my plate to cool my food and ate the resulting slop with my oversized soup spoon.

We didn't get to bring our wet, nasty duffel bags into the barracks. They lived on the rocks, and we only got ten minutes to pull out everything we needed for that night and the next day. Once we got inside our barracks building, we saw the mattresses were old and stained. Clearly, we weren't getting linen to sleep on, so I used my dirty clothes as a pillow and my towel as a blanket. One section of the B-Co area was blocked off with wall lockers so opening the locker doors would allow the women privacy for changing. The only other work done to the barracks in preparation for women was adding doors to the toilet stalls. The urinals stayed the same, but the gents who had gone through Ranger School before loved the new doors. For anyone repulsed at the idea of men and women peeing next to each other and open urinals, I assure you, none of us, male or female, cared. We were on Day Zero, and it was already just part of life. On the first night, everyone was too tired and stressed about the next day to worry about integration. No one showered. No one cared if I walked in while they were peeing. Truthfully, no student cared that a woman was even in the barracks.

We got to bed just before 2200 on Day Zero. I thought that was amazing. My first day of Ranger School was NOTHING like the blogs I read. I actually wondered if the Army made it easier because of integration.

EVENT ONE:
THE RANGER PHYSICAL FITNESS TEST

Reveille (wake up) was at 0150. If we fell asleep immediately upon arrival in the barracks and slept as long as possible, we slept for three and a half hours. Between 0150 and 0245, we conducted personal hygiene, which included cleaning the entire building and packing up any gear individuals removed from their duffel bags the night before. We were not allowed to leave anything in the barracks because, based on historical averages, the cadre expected significant attrition before the course even really started.

The first event was the Ranger Physical Fitness Test (RPFT): forty-nine push-ups, fifty-nine sit-ups, six chin-ups, and a five-mile run in forty minutes. We started at 0315, and the media frenzy was overwhelming. Suddenly, being a female Ranger hopeful was a HUGE negative. Few students actually cared inside the gates, but once we moved outside the wire surrounding Camp Rogers to take the fitness test, all bets were off. The unwanted attention made everything harder on everyone. If people had left us alone and ignored the fact that this class was different, women could have just attended the class. Instead, people looking for a fight stuck their noses and cameras where they didn't belong. There would be no leeway given on this day or any other day media were allowed near the Ranger hopefuls. Both supporters and opponents of integration were equally at fault for making this the hardest graded RPFT ever.

Rumors stated the RIs had drop quotas to support class size at various training sites throughout Ranger School. The barracks, chow hall, and training bays all had max capacities. If that was true, a significant number of people would not make it through Day One, regardless of their abilities. If enough people hadn't failed near the end of the push-up line to reach acceptable quantities, everyone who hadn't done their sets yet would fail. Rumor or not, I decided not to test that hypothesis. I channeled my best self from soccer camp as all the students began to throw elbows during lineup. I took no chances and got my ass to the front of the line. While doing my push-ups, I pancaked my boobs to the ground for every rep and hyperextended my elbows to overtly demonstrate full range of motion. If a grader didn't feel you properly executed a push-up, they did not count the rep.

When I moved from the push-up line to the sit-up line without pause, I was euphoric. As soon as I was called up, I got down and knocked out the requisite sit-ups in just over a minute. There was no talking or relaxing between events. We stayed in tight lines to avoid undue attention from the RIs. And we all definitely wanted to avoid getting culled from the herd by the circling media.

For the run, I hit the turnaround point at eighteen minutes and twenty seconds. In my mind, that was an issue because I had let myself get carried away in the moment, and I was pushing too hard. The efficient path, which I knew I had to follow, was to "barely pass" and save my energy for later. Since I would always stick out as a female student, I would never get to take it easy. Therefore, I had mentally prepared to maintain a strong and solid performance throughout the entire course, which meant saving my energy when I could. I slowed myself down on the way back, maybe a little too much. I finished the five-mile run with only ten seconds to spare. "That was too close!!" I mumbled under my breath. Then I looked back and watched guys fall over from exertion just steps before the finish line and others who were cramping on the last stretch. I was proud of my "just in time" finish, but it made me nervous to watch all those fit men fail so early in the game.

After the run, each Ranger School hopeful had to perform six dead-hang chin-ups. Those were easy. For eighty-one people, their time at Ranger School had come to an end. I was one of the 318 that made it to breakfast.

The Ranger School Way

After the RPFT, there was no time to shower, just change into our Army Combat Uniforms (ACUs). Then, the RIs introduced us to the true Ranger School way. We got smoked. What that means to people outside the military is simply that we did a level of calisthenics that would make most people sore for a week, including squats, push-ups, flutter kicks, and other strange movements not meant to be repeated in sets of twenty or thirty or one hundred. Some of these included holding our full duffel bags over our heads and doing walking lunges for an unknown distance and then being told to turn around and lunge back. I realized why we truly left our bags outside—for weights.

After our smoke session, we sprinted to the chow hall, otherwise known as the "military dining facility" (DFAC). As the crow flies, the DFAC was only about four hundred meters from the rocks, but we found a path that allowed us to run 1,200 meters to get there. We recited the Ranger Creed upon arrival. In addition to getting the words right, we also had to recite it with "proper" natural pauses. Of course, we kept screwing that up. It was inevitable. The RIs picked people they knew would mess it up. With each screw up, we got to do a little more PT. Once we finally got through all six stanzas of the creed, we completed six more chin-ups on bars right outside the DFAC, ate that same scalding-hot food in ten minutes or less, got smoked as soon as we came out for taking too long to eat, and then sprinted up a hill back to the rocks. Once we were back at the rocks, I dry heaved a few times. I damn sure didn't want to let my precious calories get away! A few others weren't so lucky.

To add to the fun, I got my period. Of course I did. Turns out, not even Depo (a birth control shot that often completely stops menstruation) was strong enough to tame the hormones produced by the stress of RAP week. Mother Nature always finds a way. This was a key argument against letting women into tough combat training and, ultimately, combat—female hygiene issues. This was one of those times when my reaction to a new stressor mattered more than the stressor itself. In other words, it wasn't a big deal that I got my period at Ranger School. What mattered was how I reacted. And no, I didn't ask for a break; I grabbed a tampon and got back in line.

Next came our equipment layout. It took over six hours and included a lot of PT. It was pretty painful, especially once our still-wet bags were all packed up. We got to sprint to and from the gym and do walking lunges, overhead squats, and more fun exercises with them. And of course, we had two minutes to repack our bags after the layout, so everything inside was a jumbled mess. The rain caused all the original containers to crumble, resulting in loose batteries, pens, etc. rolling around. Even if you had packed well, the bag dump made everything dry touch something wet. On the repack, there was no time to waterproof or fold our gear. So whenever we came back to our bags to grab the next set of items, we had to dump everything out, search like burrowing groundhogs, and then throw the slop back into the bag.

After the layout, it was time to move toward the more "tactical" requirements. Everyone got a trash bag. We filled them with items for land-nav, such as compasses, protractors, and map markers, as well as an extra set of ACUs, including boots and all the necessary undergarments. Once we secured our garbage bags, we ran to a site called the "Darby Mile" to conduct a practical exercise in preparation for our Land-Navigation test the next day.

The Darby Mile is a dirt hiking path that regularly floods. If you know anything about Georgia geology, this part of the state is primarily a clay soil. Wet, orange clay on a well-trodden path is extremely slippery, makes a huge mess, and is very taxing to walk through. It is impossible to clean off your gear and clothing. So our practical exercise on the Darby Mile was definitely NOT a refresher event to get us ready for Land Navigation. The activity was designed to add miles to already worn feet and ruin equipment. The only real benefit was validating my pace count and verifying my compass worked. A pace count is how many steps it takes to walk one hundred meters and a critical piece of knowledge for land nav. I had borrowed my compass from SGM Robbie Payne (the guy who talked me into this shit in the first place). I think he bought it when "Jesus was a private." The RIs even asked if I wanted to borrow a compass from the battalion because mine appeared to be more suitable for a Vietnam-era museum display. As it turned out, the RIs were right about that old compass. It did belong in a museum. After months of faithful, accurate service to me at Ranger School, it's now in the Smithsonian.

EVENT TWO:
COMBAT WATER SURVIVAL ASSESSMENT

After this quick exercise, we grabbed our trash bags, which were already ripping, and began running at a very brisk and painful pace in full gear to the Combat Water Survival Assessment (CWSA) course. That was exactly why I didn't want to blow myself up on the morning five-mile run. The gaggle running could barely be called a formation. One guy behind me was having a particularly difficult time. The RIs ran alongside him and told him to keep pushing.

"Keep going, Ranger! Do you want to drop? Do you want to quit? Do you want to go home to mommy?" So the kid kept pushing and made it all the way to the CWSA. Upon arrival, he turned completely white, puked a bright-green fluid, and promptly passed out in said fluid. He was a heat casualty. From there, that poor kid would be rehydrated, medically treated, and unceremoniously taken to the airport. We were now down to one hundred people in B-Co.

I couldn't let the failures of other hopefuls get to me; if I wanted to keep going, I needed to stay on top of my game, which included protecting my health and image. Just like with the fitness test, I needed to be strategic in all my actions. I was first in line to start the water obstacle course. The water cooled me, and the course was less taxing than running around carrying gear. The CWSA consisted of three events. The first event soldiers had to pass included jumping into the water wearing a Fighting Load Carrier (FLC) (a tactical vest built for carrying ammunition and other combat equipment) and carrying a dummy M4 (standard military-issue rifle with a telescoping stock), ditching the equipment once you entered the water, and then swimming fifteen meters.

We lost two more people on this event because they panicked in the water. It was infuriating. I was pissed at the individuals AND their chain of command. I wondered what the hell people were thinking coming to a school where an entire phase was called "Swamps" if they weren't comfortable wearing military gear in the water. It also really pissed me off because I heard a constant drone about women taking men's slots by getting a chance to go to Ranger School, and these two men were sent by their units completely unable to conquer their own fears on a known event on the very first day.

The inability of some to face their fears before shaving their heads and showing up to school angered me for another reason. These were supposed to be the Army's best and brightest, who could lead America's sons and daughters into combat. They better figure out how to push through their emotions. The next test struck hard at my primal trepidation toward heights, but I was mentally prepared to quiet my angst.

It started raining with gusty winds when I hit the second event. This obstacle included climbing thirty-four feet up a ladder onto an I-beam; walking "naturally" across the beam to three stair steps in the center, where each person had to casually negotiate the stairs; walking the remainder of the beam; grabbing onto a rope attached to the beam so it was almost parallel with the water below; crawling halfway out on the rope to a Ranger Tab hanging over the water; dangling by only your hands; requesting permission to drop; completing one chin-up; yelling, "Ranger!" as loud as possible; and dropping into the water. High winds blowing while thirty-four feet above the water as a fairly light person and wearing a soaked uniform changed the dynamic. I went from feeling like I might throw up from the heat to goosebumps in a matter of minutes. I actually might have enjoyed the experience if the wind wasn't making the I-beam sway and my clothes feel like a kite! I made it across, crawled on the rope, did my pull-up as effortlessly as possible, and roared, "Ranger!" as loud as I could. Mercifully,

I was granted permission to let go. Slapping the water like a sack of shit never felt so glorious.

The third and final event was basically a slide for life from a fifty-plus-foot tower. Each soldier had to carry their own metal pulley to the top. The pile of pulleys was at the end of the slide, and the bottom of the tower was two hundred meters from the pile. Because zip lines were always fun, Ranger School worked hard to ruin this one. Running from the end of the zip line to the base of the stairs and then running up the stairs carrying the metal pulley added the right amount of misery. Of course, I still loved it because I was getting to do something very few had done before me. The cadre told me to recite the first stanza of the Ranger Creed on my descent. I was pretty comfortable with that section and bellowed it out as I slid. I had my mouth open, yelling motivational stuff, as I hit the water. My teeth chattered hard when I hit the water. I fished my tongue around my mouth—I had chipped a tooth! I told no one about my tooth. I merely shut my mouth and moved out quickly. It would be hours before I could check my grin in a mirror, but I didn't care. I had passed another Ranger School hurdle. I was done with the CWSA!

It was storming pretty badly by now, but I was done with all three events. Only the swim event was mandatory, so about half the company never made it to the zip line or beam walk. After I finished, I went into the changing tents and then moved to the bleachers to eat lunch. Since training was paused for the weather, I had extra time to eat. The benefit was not lost on me. I ate every last calorie in that Meal Ready to Eat (MRE) and even licked the inside of the packaging.

My First Injury

In the afternoon, we took a ridiculous combatives class, which included some seriously watered-down knife-fighting techniques that taught people just enough to give them the confidence to get themselves killed. The RIs had to be embarrassed to teach these ineffective techniques. I finally chalked it up to just another smoke session. I really thought the training, especially the combatives skills, at Ranger School would be something amazing. So naïve.

Unfortunately for me, the combatives class wasn't just a waste of time—it also resulted in my first injury of Ranger School. When the RIs were demonstrating, they packed us in directly in front of a pit, with all three companies of Ranger students standing shoulder to shoulder and "nut to butt." At that point, the RIs told us we were too far apart, and we needed to smash it in. So we did. There was no air between bodies. It was horribly stinky, sweaty, and uncomfortable. Then, they told us to sit down. Then, they stood us back up because we had moved too far apart. We repacked ourselves like sardines and were told to sit again. I was on a lap and people, read: more than one, were on my lap. Somehow during the process, my right leg bent underneath me. Between the awkward leg angle and the additional weight, something had to give. I heard a slight pop in my knee and felt a tinge of pain. Drive on, Ranger, right?

After combatives, we were issued our Ranger Handbooks, air items, and tracking devices, called "D-stars." After the equipment issue, we were ready to prep for Land Navigation.

Holy shit! I made it through Day One.

EVENT THREE:
LAND NAVIGATION

Land Navigation was the second-highest attrition point of the school. Students had two chances to find four out of five points in a five-hour period.

Our second full day at Ranger School started at 0145. Despite less than three hours of sleep, we were all too nervous to be tired. We were on the rocks by 0215 for our breakfast MRE and then ran in formation to the Land Navigation test sight. I had a LOT in my pockets. Running in uniform with a bunch of shit in your pockets was not only annoying, it caused hotspots, abrasions, and scratches. That may not seem like a big deal, but at Ranger School, even the tiniest scratches were a serious infection threat.

On site, we got to work immediately. Eight-digit grids, when properly plotted, can get you within ten meters of your target. The RIs issued each Ranger student five sets of grid coordinates. After receiving our points, the RIs gave us fifteen minutes to plot them using white light. That was awesome and unexpected. Once 0430 hit, no more white light. We had five hours to find at least four out of the five points we were assigned. Anyone finding five out of five points would get a Major Plus. For someone comfortable with land nav, this was an easy way to give myself a cushion. But I needed to be focused on the long game. I had to decide whether a Major Plus was worth the additional time on my feet.

My knee was really unhappy, and I was limping. I found my fourth point by 0815 and had plenty of time to find my fifth. Since

I was focused on waging the long war, I decided not to risk further injury or getting lost searching for it, so I called it good enough. I headed back to the start point but went at a snail's pace to make sure I lived to fight another day. I was worried that getting back too early would yield excess attention from the RIs or they would force me to go out and try to find that fifth point. I was not the only one. There was a patch of woods behind several porta-potties about two hundred meters from the finish point, and we were stacked up hiding back there like wildebeests at a river crossing. A few brave souls napped. I checked in at the finish line at 0845. Boom! I passed another critical task at Ranger School.

This one was extremely important. The benefits were twofold. First, I knew I only had one major event remaining during RAP week. Second, and much more importantly, I wouldn't have to wander around the woods for an additional five hours the next day. I doubted the school would give us nap time while those who failed made a second attempt at the Land Navigation course, but I hoped my day wouldn't be quite as physically and mentally taxing as taking a land-nav mulligan. B-Co, my company, had a total of thirty-seven people fail the first Land Navigation test. I personally thought that was a lot, but the spring foliage did make this a difficult course.

Getting Smoked at Malvesti

After lunch, we were sent on another run. This time, it was the Darby Mile, consisting of a 1.37-mile run through natural obstructions and Georgia clay that ended in the small obstacle course called

"Malvesti." Of great importance was the fact that this obstacle course was not timed, not graded, and not a requirement to pass RAP week.

My knee was on fire by this point. I avoided looking at it, touching it, or even acknowledging it. There was no way I could medically drop from the course because someone sat on me during a fake knife-fight demonstration. But I had hit a point where I would need to confide weakness to some of my classmates for the first time in the hope we could work together.

So I looked my Ranger Buddy for this event in the eyes and said, "Hey man, I cranked my knee, and I can't do this fast. I've got to be smart and save myself for the graded events."

He replied, "Okay. We'll go as slow as we can without getting too much attention." That'll do.

The buddy team behind us wanted to go all out. They were fired up and pissed I would suggest anything less than a proper Ranger 110 percent effort. I asked them what they thought they would gain by crushing the course. I felt like my question made an impact and they were rethinking their position as we prepared to start. Right then, the RIs announced they would give any team that passed the people in front of them a Major Plus and anyone who got passed a Major Minus. Classic Ranger School conundrum, formally called the "Prisoner's Dilemma." Basically, you could really screw your buddy to benefit yourself. But if you do, everyone gets hurt in the long run if you understand the big picture. This was where the team players really stood out. Lucky for me, the team behind me finally figured out their reward for passing me would be push-ups and flutter kicks in the mud while waiting for the rest of the class to finish.

Of course, the Malvesti obstacle course was a big smoke session. Each buddy team had to complete a bunch of obstacles—rope climb, monkey bars, low crawling through nasty water—all while executing a whole lot of PT in between each event. While you waited on the teams in front of you to start negotiating an obstacle, an RI took you on an endless PT adventure while spraying you down with a water hose. We did a ton of log rolls, flutter kicks, Y-squats, and other agonizing bodyweight exercises. Jump lunges, low crawling through sawdust, and other such torture. Any failed obstacle was documented. A person was only allowed so many attempts, and failure resulted in a Major Minus. To top it all off, Malvesti was outside the gated portion of Ranger School, and the media swarmed again.

Lisa completing an obstacle at Malvesti.

My buddy had a runner's build, and even though we had paced ourselves on the run, he was completely smoked from the endless calisthenics. He couldn't get up the rope and almost didn't get across the monkey bars. The amount of attention he got for failing events was epic. Once the cadre noticed his buddy was one of the few women remaining AND I had no problems with the rope, pull-ups, or monkey bars, they really made a spectacle of him. Poor guy received nothing but anger and disgust from the RIs. After he ran slower than he could have for me, I was helpless to return the favor.

While waiting for the rest of our company to complete Malvesti, we did more calisthenics. When we weren't sprinting back and forth with a full-grown human on our shoulders, the RIs sprayed us down with hoses while we did a variety of exercises. When we weren't actively executing one of the randomly dictated movements, I shivered from the cold. When we finally finished and I collected my thoughts, I realized my knee wasn't the only joint I had to worry about. My left shoulder had started clicking somewhere between the spinning, wet monkey bars and the one thousandth pushup of the day. After graduation, I would find out I had torn a ligament in my left shoulder.

As we headed in for the night, another set of duffel bags magically disappeared from the B-Co rocks. Then the gossiping and hypothesizing started. This time, the owner of the bags was a young man who did some irreparable damage to himself on the Malvesti obstacle course. Ironically, he tore something in his shoulder. I suddenly realized how lucky I was to receive a not-so-subtle reminder that it was critical to keep quiet about any injury until it was absolutely necessary to divulge it.

Since I had already passed Land Navigation, I didn't have much to do after dinner. I did everything I could to help those who needed to go back out into the woods get ready. It felt good to do soldier stuff again.

After the second round of Land Navigation, twenty people from B-Co ultimately failed. Overall, Class 6-15 was reduced by sixty-two soldiers total. Our company was already down to seventy-six soldiers, and we still had one major graded event to go; a big one, from what I'd heard.

EVENT FOUR:
THE RUCK MARCH

After three days of constant motion, minimal sleep, and restricted calories, we started the twelve-mile road march at 0300. We had three hours to complete the march. At mile two, I was pacing much faster than my goal speed. I must have looked like death because one of the RIs yelled to me, "I hope you have a plan, Ranger. You look like you are sucking already."

I responded loudly with one of my husband's favorite responses: "Negative, Sergeant. That's just my face."

I hit mile four at fifty-nine minutes—a perfect pace. Not so fast that I was going to hit a wall, but not so slow that I was at risk of failing. At this point, I really felt like I could easily keep my fifteen-minute-mile pace for the entire walk. I felt good until the concrete turned to gravel, and the ground started sloping significantly up at mile four and a half. I lost four minutes between miles four and six. I hit the turnaround point at 1:33. I was three minutes off pace but figured I could regain it going back down the gravel hill. I was dead wrong. My right knee started aching again. Descending quickly on uneven ground was a no-go. I had to choose between injury or losing more time.

I started feeling sorry for myself. "Okay, Lisa. You can't go home because you failed the ruck."

It was 0502 when I saw the eight-mile marker. I was only two minutes behind my goal time and still had some gas left in the tank. At this point, I started seeing guys dump the water from their two-quart canteens to lighten their loads. It was a measured risk. If you got caught dumping, you could get dropped from the course for a safety violation, but every extra ounce slowed you down.

I hit mile eleven at two hours and forty-seven minutes, according to my watch. I was still two minutes behind the pace necessary to pass. Everything hurt, and the doubts crept in again. I started running—hard. I ran with all my might. I ran thinking about my amazingly supportive husband. I ran for my kids. I just kept chanting, "I shaved my head for this shit." I ran so hard I finished at 0558, two minutes before the cutoff. I finished that last mile in eleven minutes! My feet were blistered, my knee was on fire, my heart was racing, and my eyes were leaking.

I had just passed the LAST mandatory event in RAP week. I had made it through what 44 percent of Ranger hopefuls before me had failed to complete.[7] I didn't know who else was going to be at the finish line, but I did know I was one giant step closer to my goal.

INTEGRATION

Integration was going exactly the way I thought it would. Every student was too tired to care, and every RI was on pins and needles. Based on what the recycles said, our class got smoked more than any other class they had seen. Apparently, we also got less time to eat and sleep than normal. Other than our daily ten minutes for female soldiers to shower, we were treated like every other soldier in Class 6-15. I really felt like we were proving ourselves and this experience was amazing.

Three female soldiers remained in B-Co: two young lieutenants (LTs) and me. Oddly enough, we had been there four days, and I didn't even know their names. For me, this wasn't about being a woman, it was about being the best trained officer I could be, and that meant I needed to attend the best training schools the Army had to offer. I didn't want to be a "female" Ranger student. I just wanted to be a soldier at Ranger School. I thought the best way to blend in was to make friends with soldiers who weren't "special." I think most of the women felt that way because we weren't drawn

---

[7] Airborne and Ranger Training Brigade, "ARTB Course Information," Fort Benning: U.S. Army Fort Benning and The Maneuver Center of Excellence, accessed October 6, 2022, https://www.benning.army.mil/infantry/artb/Student-Information/content /PDF/ARTB%20Ranger%20Course%20Information.pdf.

to each other. We each stuck with the soldiers in our smaller groups unless it was female shower time.

Now that we had made it through RAP week, the fun could start. After showering, I grabbed my clothes but couldn't find any dry underwear, so I went commando. Almost all the guys did it, how bad could it be? Then we got smoked doing well over one hundred Y-squats. A Y-squat is simply an air squat with your hands up in the air. This movement isn't a big deal, unless you are doing it in sets of one hundred after a twelve-mile road march, after four days of "physical torture" with no underwear on. Apparently, pants rub girl parts a little differently than boy parts. After that episode, I opted for underwear for the rest of the course, even if it was nasty.

Immediately after sweating through our clean uniforms, we were taken for a medical check. The medics checked our feet. I had a strange lump growing on the inside of my left foot, probably from my boots rubbing it. It was hard, painful, and would hopefully just turn into a blister or go away in the next few days. I told them it was nothing.

During the medical check, we all stood up and pulled down our pants enough to receive two very painful shots in the butt cheek. One was penicillin, and the other...well, it was just called the "peanut butter shot." Did I mention I didn't have any underwear on? The medic got a special treat with this first integrated class!

While getting my shots, I also got my first glimpse of what the outside world thought about women at Ranger School. After literally showing my ass, the one female medic in the room gave me what appeared to be an evil glare, but then she whispered, ever so softly, "You fucking go, girl." That was such a perfect encapsulation of my journey so far. Other people's emotional reactions to my journey were so visceral, I couldn't tell the supporters from the haters.

We spent the rest of the day in classes. No one could sit still for long. Everyone's butt hurt from those damn shots. It felt like someone had injected a golf ball into my right cheek.

The OAs were present for all these classes. It was ridiculous. Did the women who volunteered for the first-ever integrated Ranger School really need special supervision while sitting in a class? What did the Army think we were going to do, flash the RIs and ask for our "Go"? As the class progressed, one of the OAs started "advising" me on tactics during a rehearsal with my squad. Really? After I received my instruction from the OA, I heard one of the other female students whisper, "Cut your fucking hair, then you can talk."

I'm not mad at the ladies who volunteered to be OAs. They raised their hands to complete a task the Army required. I accepted what the OAs were trying to do, but I never really liked the program. In those early days, most of the female Ranger hopefuls would have run the OAs out of camp if we could.

On Day Four, we were issued weapons and then packed our rucks with very few items. These items were supposed to hold us over for the next two weeks. I didn't believe this small handful of items would be enough for the duration of our Camp Darby training, but I didn't want to pack any more than I absolutely had to. The biggest argument I had heard against women at Ranger School was we weren't physically strong enough to hump our own packs and carry our own weight. Although I didn't believe that to be true, I wasn't about to add extra stuff and prove all the naysayers right. After packing our rucks for Darby, we put our wet, nasty duffel bags in the back of a semitrailer for storage.

I constantly felt the need to validate the women who remained in Ranger School because I knew there would be plenty of doubters. Comments about strength and ability continually flowed through the back of my mind. By the end of Day Four, I knew the stats for all the female students. I asked around and wrote everything in my pocket notebook because the dwindling female ranks made my success even more critical. It seemed like everyone was tracking us. B-Co lost one female student to the RPFT, one to Land Navigation, and two to the Ruck March. That 57 percent fail rate was higher than the 44 percent reported average RAP-week failures.[8] Overall, Class 6-15 had gone from nineteen women to eight. I didn't know most of the women in my class, but I assumed we were all similar, and I started to wonder if we all got together, would we clash or click?

As we closed out RAP week, it became apparent being a female student didn't matter nearly as much as being a prepared student who spent time and energy focusing on individual skills and fitness prior to shaving your head and stepping into the arena. Somehow, the RIs were shocked at the remaining eight of us, while my classmates accepted the reality that I was ready to tackle this challenge. Just. Like. Them.

---

[8] Airborne and Ranger Training Brigade, "ARTB Course Information."

CHAPTER 3

CHANGING STANDARDS

Darby 1

Day 6–Day 20/April 24–May 9

> *"God, grant me the ability to ignore the people I cannot change;*
> *the courage to keep trying to change the people I can;*
> *and the wisdom to know the difference."*

> —My Ranger School serenity prayer

Prior to women "invading" Ranger School, the first topic of conversation was *if* women could hold their own. The second, and much more dominant concern, seemed to be whether or not the standards would change to accommodate the fairer sex. Would we have lighter packs, get more showers, or have a "female" physical fitness standard? I can confidently declare the standards did, in fact, change. They got harder, and everyone knew it.

I was so excited to leave Camp Rogers and RAP week behind me. I was full of confidence and counting down the days until graduation. I thought RAP week, specifically the RPFT five-mile run, would be my big hurdle. I figured if I passed the first four days, I should be able to make it straight through. I mean, I have several deployments under my belt and am a West Point grad, and small-unit tactics hadn't changed significantly since Jesus was a private. All I had to do now was stay healthy.

Unfortunately, I quickly realized my confidence was misplaced. We began Day Seven with classes and then headed to the infamous "Darby Queen" obstacle course. I wanted a tall partner because there was one obstacle that required two people to work together to ascend to the top. It was six layers of shelves that were six to seven feet apart. Each Ranger Buddy team needed to scramble up the outsides of the platform to get to the next layer and then come back down. I grabbed the biggest soldier I could find. I figured we would fly up that obstacle.

We made it to "Tarzan" without issue. This obstacle had a balance beam walk and then monkey bars made out of logs. In the waiting area, there were four camera crews. That should have been foreshadowing for me about the suck we were about to endure, but I was still oblivious and believed that somehow my quest for an elite training experience was not going to be made into a dog-and-pony show. I was SO wrong!!!! The media's presence annoyed the RIs, and they took it out on the class. I don't know if the military allowed those camera crews to be there or the media simply found a way in, but whoever allowed those cameras to infiltrate our training area should be fired.

Normally, if you got to an obstacle and there were already people on it, you just jogged in place while waiting your turn. But the RI in charge of Tarzan decided fireman-carry races up a nearby hill would determine who got to attempt the obstacle he was guarding. Once I surveyed the situation, I didn't feel so smart anymore for purposefully pairing myself with the biggest dude in our class. The RI made me carry my partner's big ass up the hill, and he carried me down, every time. We tried taking turns on who carried who on the uphill but were quickly scolded and rearranged back to the original, dictated order. We were never last in the races, but we couldn't win. My partner weighed well over two hundred pounds. We continued to run carrying each other until every other team and the cameras moved on. Only then were we allowed to complete the obstacle. I felt so bad for him. A lesser man would have hated women at Ranger School after that event.

Buddy carries from Hell during the obstacle course at Camp Darby.

One of the biggest arguments against women in the infantry was that a woman could not pick up a full-grown man and carry him off the battlefield. My weight hovers around 145 pounds, and I can lift more than the average person my size. How would a 145-pound male soldier fare sprinting uphill with a two-hundred-pound Ranger Buddy for about an hour? No smaller male soldiers were forced to carry their larger counterparts uphill repeatedly that day, so I may never know. The discussion should be about strength and ability, not gender.

Because we were now in the back, we had to pick up a third Ranger Buddy who was removed from the course when he showed significant signs of dehydration. He received an IV and was sent back in to attempt to finish the course. That was another issue with being at the back: if something happened, there was no stopping for a second and then getting moved to the back of the line. I was already the caboose.

At some point, we had to prisoner of war crawl. That meant moving on our bellies with our hands "tied" behind our backs, basically slinking across the ground like worms. Then we had to drag a "casualty" through the dirt who was holding onto our necks while we crawled. There were a variety of other drags, drills, and pulls that resulted in sand, dirt, mud, and woodchips going into any available space on our bodies and in our uniforms. Once we finally made it to the partner obstacle I had been concerned about, the RIs sent my "big buddy" forward with someone else, and I was paired with the heat casualty. He was my size, and after the day he had had so far, he wasn't as strong as I was. I ended up having to do a lot of the heavy lifting on an obstacle made for tall people.

But there was a benefit: I learned to trust my own strength and skill. That was a lesson I thought I had learned years earlier, but it was good to have a reminder. By proving I could do it with someone smaller and more exhausted than me, I showed myself and all the RIs watching that this tiny, wrinkly, old package still had a few surprises.

STARTING TACTICS

We had a few minutes to change after the obstacle course. There is no way to describe the smell or sight of us. We had another quick

MRE, and then we were off to the Ranger Training Tasks (RTT) test. I failed two tasks, resulting in my second Major Minus for the day. Out of the entire 6-15 Ranger School class, only one guy got all the RTT tasks correct, and two more got only one wrong. They received a Minor Minus. Everyone else in the class earned a Major Minus. I was not alone, but I was pissed and getting frustrated.

The soldiers who had recycled from the previous class and joined our class at Darby didn't have to take RTT, and all they kept saying was how much harder we had it than they did the last time. Really? This chapped my ass because prior to Ranger School, I'd heard so much about "the standard" and how me being there was going to jeopardize the precious standard. There was no way the school would "change the standard." That day, the *standard* seemed to be whatever the cadre felt like they wanted it to be, and if it was changed, it had gotten harder, not easier—especially for the female contingent. That was by far my hardest day in Ranger School to date, and I had no idea if it was going to get better or worse.

Luckily, we got a short reprieve that evening. Around 2000, we forced down a quick MRE and then headed off to a hill where we would sit in the grass and listen to scripture. It was my first real chance to sit, think, and breathe. My grandmother had died a month earlier, and her ashes had been brought back to Wisconsin. As I sat in the service with my boots off, trying to stay awake enough to listen to the preacher, I realized today was the day my entire family was saying their final goodbyes to Grandma Peplinski, and I was missing it. I pulled my hat a little further down over my eyes and shed a few tears. Honestly, the service was pretty crappy. It didn't resonate with me at all, but the time to reflect, mentally say my goodbyes to Grandma, and refresh my perspective after failing miserably earlier in the day got my mind right. At the service's conclusion, the preacher's assistant handed out white bread with a chunk of peanut butter on it. It was like manna from heaven!

During the service, my feet started itching like crazy. This wasn't an itch you could ignore. This was one of those "take out your pocketknife to scratch" types of itches. I removed my boots and socks for a bit. "Shit. That's not good." Even though it was getting dark, I could see how poorly my feet were faring.

PRACTICAL EXERCISES: CARRYING THE GUN

On Day Nine, Practical Exercises (PEs) began. Pes included running through all or part of a mission set without getting graded but while the Ris watched and gave feedback. During our first PE, we planned our first mission as a squad. This made me happy because we could finally start working together and building rapport. We would fail or succeed based on our ability to support each other. It was an excellent learning experience. I learned a bit more about applied tactics, putting what I already knew academically into action. This was the first time since cadet training that I was a member of a squad, just part of the team and not leading it. Sometimes, following is harder than leading. Actually, I think following is always harder than leading. I had to figure that piece out if I wanted to help my squad succeed.

The cadre apparently wanted to help me learn to be a member of the team and assigned me the role of the M240 gunner. The M240 by itself weighs twenty-seven pounds and comes with a lot of extras, such as rounds, a spare barrel, and a tripod. Everyone snickered when my roster number was called to carry the gun. "At least they are fucking you from the beginning, Jaster. No hiding that one." I constantly had the choice to read into shit and get bitter, or suck it up and drive on. Be the better soldier. Don't complain. Do everything you are asked and more. I'm sure that's in the Ranger Creed somewhere. Maybe the third stanza, "I will shoulder more than my share of the task whatever it may be, one hundred percent and then some." Time to suck it up, buttercup, and head out for some good Ranger training!

While we were out on mission, there was not a lot of cover. A light, cool drizzle started. I had to go to the bathroom. And soon! But I was literally tied to that damn twenty-seven-pound gun. The schoolhouse rules said I could not leave my Ranger Buddy, and I could not go outside the perimeter. All the guys just took a couple steps away from their fighting position, got up on a knee, and watered a tree. Part of my mandatory packing list included something called a Female Urinary Device (FUD). I had never seen one before and definitely never used one. It appeared I was not going to be able to keep that trend going. I moved as far away from my M240 as my dummy cord (a string tied to me on one end and the gun on the other) would allow, unbuttoned my fly, and attempted to use a funnel to pee while in the kneeling position. This soon became known as my "FUD Fail." My Assistant Gunner (AG) acted like he didn't notice I had peed all over myself. I decided to "accidentally" spill my entire two-quart canteen on myself. I had to resort to hydro-theatrics because they will kick you out of Ranger School in an instant for dumping water.

Minutes later, it started raining. I was relieved at first since my FUD Fail would no longer be obvious. That relief was short-lived. The Georgia clay meant the rain wouldn't soak into the ground. If we stayed here, it was going to be a long, cold night! It actually got worse from there. The rain must have been the lead edge of a front because the temperature dropped dramatically. We laid on the wet ground, getting beamed with cold chunks of precipitation. The cadre did not allow us to put on waterproof gear or warm clothes. As part of my Ranger School education, I learned snivel gear, anything meant to protect you from the elements, was just stuff you carried for added weight in your ruck. You don't actually get to use it.

Just as I started to sneak my poncho out of my bag to lay over me, we received the order to get up and move out. We were headed to our patrol base. The ground under our feet felt like a Slip 'N Slide. Since this was just a training event and not a graded exercise, the RIs let us walk on the roads. Although we thought this would be faster and easier on our bodies, that was far from the truth. It was awful. The path went up and over undulating hills rather than weaving through the terrain. The mud was slick and unforgiving, with no underbrush to add traction or soften our falls. Then the sun started to set. As soon as we mounted our night-vision goggles (NVGs) to our helmets, our world became green and two-dimensional. The combination of our hot breath and the cold rain fogged both the NVG lenses and our mandatory safety-goggle lenses. Our socks were heavy with water. My feet started slipping inside my boots, and my boots slipped on the clay.

As I tried to carry the M240 up and down hills, I became extremely unbalanced and started misstepping. I was falling forward rather than backward. I would jut out my elbows or knees when I fell to make sure I didn't come down squarely on the weapon. As bad as I was, I was far from the worst bull marching through the china shop. The storm was loud, but my squad was significantly louder. Mercifully, the noises coming from the calamity covered any sound my AG made since I was certain he was laughing his ass off. To my surprise, he was extremely empathetic. Later, he admitted he was the M240 gunner in his unit. He found it both refreshing and hilarious that his first Ranger School mission included supporting an officer getting firsthand knowledge of what he dealt with daily. I gave him respect and a hearty handshake later that night when we made it to base camp—alive and unbroken.

Once we arrived at our designated patrol base site, I felt a slight burning sensation in my feet, and the itching from church returned. I pondered trying to change my socks or at least take off my boots to see how bad my feet were but thought better of it. No reason to waste time on something I couldn't really impact.

We, my AG and I, laid down in our assigned spot, a cozy mud puddle for two, and set up for the night. Every other Ranger Buddy pair in the perimeter laid so close together you couldn't distinguish one soldier's camouflage from the next. There were small "people" piles all around the camp. I fully expected to do the same to stay warm and get some rest; people in the military snuggle to sleep if the temps dip below sixty. But my buddy was worried his wife would be mad if he "cuddled" with me. You've got to be shitting me! The only person who couldn't get a guy to snuggle was the woman. Eventually, I stopped chasing him around our mud pit and just laid on my side convinced I was going die that night from hypothermia because my Ranger Buddy would rather snuggle with another dude than piss off his wife.

It was a shitty day. But Day Nine was officially done, and I happily crossed it off in my notebook. Now, time to get after Day Ten. Seeing the days go into double digits brought a short-lived high that ended when I finally looked at my feet. They had started bleeding, and the callouses on the balls of my feet were peeling back in one large sheet. I also now had not one but two sets of wet boots.

BEING A SMART RANGER

Our next stage was going through the motions while an RI played a key role in the mission to demonstrate what the standard looked like. During instructor-assisted squad recon, we needed to prep as if we were staying in a patrol base. The RIs gave us some leeway on how we did our planning. I quickly discovered what I brought to the team. I may not be the smoothest person in the woods, but my military and life experience made planning easy. I knew how to quickly develop a tactical plan from reading an Operations Order (OPORD) and looking at a map. I could write up critical parts of the graded brief in minutes, when it took others the better part of an hour. I could dictate the five required paragraphs of an order with minimal prep in a way that even the most inexperienced soldiers understood. There were strong Rangers and smart Rangers. I wanted to be both, but I was leading with my brain, and it was appreciated by all.

On the first day of graded patrols, I volunteered to carry the M249, but I was subbed out halfway through the mission and assigned to be the new squad leader. I was getting graded! I definitely got a "No Go" for this mission since I got into a shootout with OP4 and "died," but I had so much fun! I knew I would get another shot at a graded patrol, and I felt confident I would pass the next one.

After mission completion, the RI gave us a new grid for our patrol base. It was over four kilometers away. The group was already spent and totally defeated from a hard day. My feet were getting worse, and this longer movement was wearing on me as well. At one point, when everyone was getting overly angry, I called a halt. I told the squad to drop their rucksacks and face outward, pulling security and getting their minds right. It was a terrible tactical decision, but it was great for morale. Since I had already failed my patrol, this was a huge reward to my team with no short-term risk.

Once we arrived at the patrol base, I failed as a tactical leader once again. I had never seen a squad-level patrol base. It wasn't something the real army does, and the one class scheduled to review this technique was rained out. We buzzed through the concept during the classroom portion because the RIs knew it was a useless skill. I guessed at every step. When we finally finished, it was late, and I had needed a lot of guidance. I felt like an idiot and knew in my heart that everyone was judging me for my severe lack of tactical ability. I just negated all the good I did with my nontactical rest stop. I would have to prove myself by adding value in every other way possible if I was going to stay in my team's good graces.

But I didn't have a chance to worry or wonder for long. Just as we started working on personal hygiene, the marine in our squad laid on the ground, saying he couldn't move. I ran up the hill a significant distance to try to find an RI. The situation deteriorated quickly. We had to put the marine on the SkedCo (a plastic sheet used as a litter to carry casualties). It was extremely disappointing how long it took for the 4th Ranger Battalion medical staff to arrive. The sick marine just kept getting worse. I talked to him the entire time about his family, his hobbies, etc. After sitting with him on the road for well over thirty minutes, we moved him to the cadre campsite, where they had a fire going, because no matter how many of our blankets and jackets we threw on him, he couldn't seem to warm up. He started having severe pain in his side as well. The Field Litter Ambulance (FLA) didn't come until more than an hour after we called them. We later found out the marine had kidney stones.

Once the medics took him away, I headed back down the hill to the patrol base, where the rest of the squad was waiting. We ate our MREs and completed a mission After Action Review (AAR), and then we went to sleep, non-tactically. We were exhausted from real-world and mission concerns. We didn't get to lay down until 0500, which was our normal wake-up time. The RIs let us sleep until 0730, which seemed great, except it put us way behind for the next day's mission.

STILL CARRYING THE BIG GUN

On our thirteenth day at Ranger School and our third day in the field, the cadre assigned the M240 to me again! We were conducting another recon, which meant carrying the M240 sucked just a bit more because there was very little chance of actually getting to fire it and expend ammunition, keeping my load fairly heavy. This time, more than one of my squad mates voiced opinions that the RIs were trying to break me. Because I needed to stay positive, I just told myself a major has more responsibility in battle and therefore should be held to a higher standard. I knew it was bullshit, but I had gotten through a lot of crap at various points in my life with positive self-talk.

To add insult to injury, my feet were getting worse. I had to dampen my socks prior to removing them to limit the amount of skin that came with the socks. When the medic looked at my feet, he actually asked if I wanted to medical drop and start over as a recycle in the next class. That was not a good sign. All of the skin came off my left pinky toe in a solid sleeve. To say it was disgusting would be a bit of an understatement.

Mercifully, while we were in the Objective Rally Point (ORP), the OP4 probed our perimeter. I was alert and blasted the HELL out of those guys. The mission's Bravo Team Leader (BTL), someone who had proven beyond a doubt to be the laziest soldier I have ever met, was in charge of the ORP. Due to my violence of action and the performance of his security team, he definitely got a "Go," allowing him to move on to the next stage without much effort on his part. Ranger School was anything but fair.

On Day Fourteen, I still had the M240 from the previous day's missions. Everyone was spent. No one cared that during the entire field problem, I was either carrying one of the bigger weapons or in a leadership role. And there was no way in hell I would admit any weakness at this point. So I put my head down and focused on placing one bloody foot in front of the other. Mission first... whatever.

I was limping really badly by this time and started developing blisters on my right ankle from my change in gait. The skin on my right pinky toe also separated in one chunk, just as my left one had. The only saving grace was a small piece of live flesh keeping the skin on my right foot. That skin barrier decreased the pain from the foot rubbing the inside of my boot. I also had a small scratch on my right wrist from a tree branch that got infected almost immediately because we were so dirty and nasty. My pasty, white body was covered in bruises and heat rash, with a touch of sunburn on my constantly exposed hands and neck. My elbows had deep scrapes, and my leg hair was fully grown in. Damn sexy.

I glanced at my list of days. Two weeks done. *I can do this.*

SQUAD LEADER

After refitting and having a day of retraining, we got our job assignments for the first day of our next field problem. I would be the squad leader for bay planning in the morning. They gave me a job square in my wheelhouse! Easy "Go" for me!

Big breath, here we go. I walked into the coordination meeting with my notes and OPORD prepared. All my squad assembled around me to get their brief.

As I was about to start, the RI announced, "Jaster, there's a few changes." He handed me a piece of paper. "Adjust your plan and brief." He changed everything about my mission on the spot. Everything! The start point, mission location, patrol base, infiltration method—everything. On the spot, while being graded and in front of the other Ranger students and five very alert RIs, I came up with new routes (primary and alternate), Ambulance Exchange Points (AXPs), artillery targets, Casualty Collection Points (CCPs), check points—everything. I saw a lot of eyebrows raise. Boom. I absolutely smoked the Warning Order (WARNO) and OPORD. I received a ton of compliments from both my peers and the RIs. "Seems like you might know what you are doing, Jaster," I heard someone say. *Damn straight I do. I definitely got my "Go."*

During our movement, we were hit by artillery simulators five times, which is excessive by anyone's standard. Two, maybe three, was the norm. My squad ran all over the place, having to change direction in an attempt to elude the "enemy." There was one rough patch where I lost control of my squad for a minute. I screwed up big time calling a break contact. Normally, you do not break contact, but we were divided over a road near an open field. The A-team leader, even though he heard me, decided to flank instead.

The RI standing right by me snorted, "Jaster, your team leader fucked you." That A-team leader was pretty squared away, but he got really anxious under pressure.

Once we finally stopped, the RI asked me to pinpoint our location on the map. It took me less than sixty seconds to give him a grid (we were not using GPS). "We're right here." The RI was a bit shocked. I think he expected me to be completely disoriented, and he didn't know how to react when I didn't crumble under the pressure.

I think the only way I am going to succeed at Ranger School is by winning each RI over, one at a time, I thought.

During my AAR, the RI said my Troop Leading Procedures (TLPs) were the best he's seen in three years as a lane walker. I made a few mistakes, but they were based on my lack of familiarity with being in the field conducting small-unit tactics. The RI responded to some of my self-diagnosed concerns by saying I would have plenty of time to fix them in Mountains. Hell yeah, baby!

I was happy. Everyone talked about my mission planning and execution. I was moving on to Mountains Phase. I got to sit back and be a "member of the team" for the next two and a half days. They could even give me the M240 again, and I wouldn't be mad. We would come out of the field on Wednesday. The recycles told me we wouldn't sleep at all that night, and we'd head back to Camp Rogers on Thursday. We would get an eight-hour pass on Friday. Some of us made plans to go to Dairy Queen to kill some Blizzards. After that, maybe IHOP! Then, on Saturday, we'd be headed to the mountains. Life was good.

NEVER GIVE UP

On our sixteenth day at the school, we conducted a helicopter (helo) infiltration. Normally, I would think that was fun, but I just wanted to sleep. This was the first time the sleep deprivation really hit me. Maybe my adrenaline had been keeping me going and my good patrol had relaxed me a bit.

To make sure Ranger School didn't permanently break the soldiers, medics came out daily to check our feet and ask us about any other health issues we might have. By this time, most people had received something for a rash, an infection, or both. The skin on my feet literally tore apart like tissue paper. In the areas where it remained intact, it was almost transparent. I swear you could see my heart beating through my soles. After looking at my feet, an RI decided to call a nine-line Medical Evacuation (MEDEVAC) to have me removed from training. I stood right by him while he was on his radio. When I heard the voice on the other end of the radio ask if the soldier wanted to be evacuated or if the RI was requesting the MEDEVAC, I broke all military bearing and started yelling that I was staying. It was a bit of a fight, but the RI couldn't have me trucked out if I refused to say I was in any pain. He couldn't do anything, so I stayed with my squad. When we started moving again, the RI allowed my entire squad to walk the road and head directly to the patrol base because he was so worried about my feet. I never slowed down, and my guys loved me for being the reason their walk was cut short.

The last day of patrols was here. I was on cloud nine, dreaming about Dairy Queen and getting to know my new friends better during our pass. When the RIs showed up, I was assigned as the Alpha Team Leader (ATL), a graded position. I was absolutely shocked because I knew I already had a "Go." The recycles assured me it was normal to pair a good soldier who was competent and had their "Go" with someone who was having a really rough time tactically. It gave that person the best opportunity to pass.

The ATL was in charge of the route and the terrain model. During the order's process, the RI never even looked at my terrain model or route plan. He didn't even ask questions about my part of the order, which was a solid nonverbal validation that I had my "Go" and wasn't getting graded today. Even though I was not getting graded, I needed to do my best to ensure the others were set up for success.

I was in the lead during our movement and expertly navigated my squad through the woods. When we received indirect fire, I kept the team and squad together well. They hit us with artillery simulators (arty) so many times in a row we needed to change directions. I kept my bearing and was able to get us back on azimuth without any issues. Azimuth is just the direction, usually guided by a compass reading, the team needs to travel. The only negative AAR comment I received was that while we were reacting to contact, the squad leader tried to take over my team. He just got too excited, and rather than giving me instructions and leading the squad, he fell into his comfort zone and tried to lead my team.

The moment of truth arrived. We stood in formation as the RIs called out numbers. If your number was called, you recycled.

My mind drifted to my Dairy Queen Blizzard, barely listening, when they called my number. Nope. Not possible. Every damn person in my squad dropped their jaw and stared at me. It didn't take long to see that all the female students were either recycled or dropped. Apparently, I failed patrols. Fuck! I was pissed. I could not understand how I didn't get a "Go." How could this be true after all the praise I received from my squad mates and the graders on each lane? What the fuck was I supposed to improve if the RI told me it was the best he'd ever seen? I get that life isn't fair but fuck this.

As we started loading up at Camp Darby, I volunteered to be the class leader. I thought it would help keep my head in the game and maybe the bitterness at bay. I had to focus on something. I had always found if I cheer for those around me and focus on helping them through the suck, then my pain, discomfort, and anguish all but disappear. My fastest run times were when I tried to get someone else to move faster.

I was able to call Allan and talk for a whole two minutes. That was a difficult call to make. Luckily, when I told him I was recycled, he merely demonstrated concern for how I was doing. Nothing more, nothing less. God, I love that man. I later found out he knew before I did.

I had a chance to talk to some of the other women once we got back to Camp Rogers. Shaye Haver was another woman in my company. She was also a West Pointer and a badass to boot. Haver was the real deal. She felt pretty strongly she successfully executed her patrols as well. It wasn't arrogance; she had a squad full of people and cues from RIs telling her she did a great job and deserved to move on. That story sounded familiar.

BY THE NUMBERS

I came to grips with the inevitable when the recycles all transitioned to Vaughan's Platoon. Vaughan's Platoon was the name given to everyone who was at Ranger School but not in an active class. There were 108 people in Vaughan's; our group was so big the cadre called us "Vaughan's Company." It was the largest group of recycles anyone had ever seen.

The Battalion Commander, who was responsible for all students, RIs, and support staff at Camp Darby and Camp Rogers, told us the class failed because of a lack of teamwork. I guess I know how he spun recycling all eight women to his superiors and the media. Since we passed the physical requirements, they needed an excuse. According to this ass clown, women were strong enough, but their presence degraded cohesion. Shockingly, he never mentioned how the grading standards for RTT were harder than ever before, there were additional observers on missions when women were graded, and "standards" were followed with more rigor than any recycle had ever seen before. Yup, it was just that women screw things up by existing. Oh, the mystical alchemy of the bro bond was once again in play.

I joined my new best friends for the next few days and tried to stay calm and humble. We spent a lot of the day just sitting outside on a grassy patch on our bags. Everyone was worn out, but no one dared sleep. We had not been given any food for lunch, so we just sat, folded clothes, and traded supplies.

All that time sitting opened the door for conspiracy theories. A lot of the guys recycling were ones perceived to be close with a female soldier. All the guys hoped they didn't get a squad with a female student once Ranger Class 7-15 started up. It was crazy. The guys we fought our "Ranger School Battles" next to respected us and had no problems working with us, but the school atmosphere was destroying the integration process. The men recycling from Class 6-15 were furious and talking about calling congressmen and newspapers during their passes. They speculated the cadre failed an inordinate number of guys so it would not look as bad when they failed all the women. As ridiculous as it sounded, I didn't have a counter argument. Only one thing was different this time than with all the other classes over the last sixty-five years, and it was us. I just kept my mouth shut. All the crying in the world wasn't going to get me to Mountains.

One of my buddies collected data from each of the recycles and worked the numbers.

A1-1 5/17, 2 females (29%)	B1-1 5/18, 1 female (28%)	C1-1 14/17 (82%)
A1-2 2/18, 1 female (11%)	B1-2 6/18, 1 female (33%)	C1-2 10/18 (56%)
A1-3 14/18 (78%)	B1-3 9/18 (50%)	C1-3 10/16 (63%)
A2-1 5/17 (29%)	B2-1 10/17 (59%)	C2-1 6/16, 1 female (38%)
A2-2 9/17 (53%)	B2-2 5/17, 1 female (29%)	C2-2 3/19, 1 female (16%)

He calculated that squads with women had a 25 percent "Go" rate, whereas all-male squads had an average "Go" rate of 59 percent. It was as if a different standard was applied to the female squads. The argument was that the women were destroying group cohesion, causing the entire team to fail. Except six out of the eight women peered high, indicating their male classmates respected them and found they were adding value to the small unit. Those who suggested the failure rates were because we just didn't have the tactical skills, field craft, or small-unit leadership ability were just being intellectually dishonest. The idea that somehow junior enlisted soldiers with eighteen months in the army possessed these skills, but it was completely absent in these seasoned women, was inconceivable.

Even the highest "Go" rate for a squad with women was well below the Darby average. Everyone who had previously attended

Ranger School said the standards for our class were significantly higher than ever before. Our class started with 399 soldiers, marines, airmen, and foreign officers. We received seventy-one recycles from the previous class. Eighty failed the RPA, four failed the CWSA, sixty-two failed Land Navigation, and forty-nine failed the Ruck March. Class 6-15 also had forty-nine drops due to twelve medical, two administrative, four Serious Observation Reports (SORs), and thirty-one boards (individuals who went in front of the cadre after failing an event and were either retained or kicked out of this iteration). At the end, only 115 out of the entire group (399 plus 71 recycles) moved on to Mountains. And three more dropped due to lack of motivation (LOM). One hundred and eight remained to start over.

Later, I chatted with the Charlie Company (C-Co) first sergeant about the situation. He said the mass killings (recycles and drops) were due to everyone being nervous about being "judged," so the RIs graded completely by the book, leaving no room for "common sense" or judgment calls. I had mixed feelings on that one. Maybe they should always judge by the book—or maybe not. Regardless, the "Ranger Standard" can't be a moving target. That was bad for the school and soul crushing for the soldiers living it.

I guess all those guys worried about the standards changing when women entered the course were right. Just not the way everyone expected. The standards did change. They got harder.

CHAPTER 4

THE CRAZY 8

Recycle

May 9–May 14

I dubbed the women who had made it through RAP week into Darby the "Crazy 8." This was the first time I really spoke with most of these ladies. Each came with an impressive resume and great story. I quickly realized it was a phenomenal group of women.

We told a few stories and laughed like we were at a slumber party as we cross-leveled gear and field supplies with one another. I would nod and interject on occasion but stayed quiet at first. There was a preexisting bond between them because they had moved to Fort Benning together after completing RTAC to train for Ranger School. Unfortunately, I had not had the ability to take that much time off work to train, nor had I felt I could do that to my family, so I initially felt like an outsider among them.

I asked a lot of questions, learning each of their stories. I had never been in a room full of alpha females. I didn't know what to expect. Our discussions could be competitive, calculative, or bonding. After a while, I told my own tall tale or two. One day, just as we were walking out for dinner formation, one of the captains walked up to my cot and simply said, "Damn—I bet you were wild when you were younger."

I felt a kinship with the Crazy 8. I was becoming ingrained in soldiering again and remembering why it was so hard for me to leave active duty in 2007. The weird thing here, as a recycle at Ranger School, was I had seven other women who were just as crazy as I was and all alphas, yet none of us felt competitive toward one another. I felt protective of these women. During the recycle, I tried not to read anything about Ranger School or any of the articles about the women. I was informed by some officers stationed at Benning that the plan was to keep all the women together, fail or pass. Maybe that's why Shaye and I didn't move on. Who knows? I did not want to hear that there was some master plan for us. Just give me a damn meritocracy, and I would be fine, pass or fail.

No one seemed bitter, and everyone was supportive. I wished women in every field could support each other like this. At thirty-seven, I found a true sisterhood at Ranger School. Ha! Funny thing to say: "a sisterhood at Ranger School."

Despite the camaraderie, we all felt Ranger School wearing on us. Physically, I recuperated pretty quickly. My feet were almost completely covered in actual skin now. I still had a few scabs, and the skin was thin, but at least it was there. Of course, we would insert into the next class soon and start running around in wet boots again, so I needed them to be closer to 100 percent healed. I had lost a lot of weight; my face was gaunt, and for the first time in my life, my abs rocked. More worrisome than my feet, however, was my mental state: an animosity was slowly festering within me. The idea that none of the women passed a single patrol ground on me, especially since I knew how well two-thirds of my patrols went. Mentally, I probably needed a little more time to recover.

STARTING OVER

May 10, 2015, was my twenty-first day at Ranger School, not counting Day Zero. I should have been starting Mountains; instead, I watched the new students arrive. Happy Mother's Day to me.

Though I was feeling low, I had to admit there were a few perks to being a recycle. I got to change my clothes daily—all of them. No swapping out fresh maxi pads because I couldn't change my underwear. I showered every day, sometimes twice per day. I even slept.

There were also a lot of negatives. My mind wasn't filled with the stress of the next patrol, and my body wasn't exhausted from constantly standing and moving under load. Without those external forces, I had time to think. My heart ached, and I missed my people back home. I started wondering if the 4th Ranger Training Battalion (RTB) cadre would actually allow any of us to make it to Mountains. I *had* to believe I was going to get a fair shake this time around and move on to the next phase. Otherwise, what the hell was I doing this for?

I wanted to be here. I knew there were so many critical reasons to stay, and my kids had to be part of my motivation, not my distraction. When we were busy, there was no time to worry about anything, especially things that didn't impact Ranger School, but when we had light duty, my mind became my enemy. I realized Ranger School would force me to recycle each phase, IF they let me pass at all. I had come here thinking I was in and out in nine weeks. Nothing was that hard here. But based on my calculations, and my fairly negative view of things, I wouldn't graduate until Class 9-15. That was in September! That was five full months separated from those I held most dear. It was a bit overwhelming. I was suddenly overcome by the intense suspicion we really were going through a social experiment like all the haters said. Were we just here for a liberal agenda and never had a chance to succeed? Serenity prayer.

Day Twenty-Two became my new Day One. I thought of it as D2-1 for my second go at Darby. Class 7-15 started, and we helped out with their RPFT. The event was so much calmer without the extra attention. The RIs yelled a lot less. I was on the sidelines, but everyone there felt the difference from just three weeks earlier.

Lots of recycles were barely feigning effort, but all the women were pushing hard. We still had a spotlight on us, maybe even more now than when we first arrived. Three weeks into this endeavor, having to be constantly "on" and never getting to just hunker down and blend in wore on each of us. I hoped the female novelty would fade as the course rolled on. I told myself, "By now, people have got to understand we're not just going to fall down, break, cry, or quit."

When I got disappointed, depressed, or disheartened, I told myself, "Holy shit, I'm at fucking Ranger School." That helped. If someone told me I would be one of the first women at Ranger School fifteen years after commissioning, I would have laughed right in their face. The mantra of "I GET to be here" reminded me attending Ranger School WAS the end state. Having the opportunity to go to the same school my male peers had attended over a decade before was a feat in and of itself. Plus, my dad went to this school, and I thought about him here as a twenty-something soldier. I wanted my tab more than words could express.

Unfortunately, most days I felt like we were not going to advance, so the positive thought I snatched out of this experience was that five to six hundred Ranger hopefuls, RIs, media people, O/As, etc., saw us ladies keep up physically, hold up mentally, and perform tactically. The Crazy 8 might never earn our tabs, but we definitely earned respect and influenced the minds of future leaders. For the recycles, myself and the Crazy 8 included, this was it. In almost all cases, students only get to retry a phase once. If you can't pass a phase after two attempts, it's curtains for your tab chase. Time to pack your shit and come up with a good story for why you didn't make it through Ranger School.

CHAPTER 5

THE SHIT SHOW

Darby 2

May 14–May 30

Darby Two, Day Four. Time to join Ranger Class 7-15. This time around, I was assigned to A-Company (A-Co).

When I joined my new squad, I was optimistic. Restarting was so much easier than starting from scratch! No RAP week!!!! I was relatively fat, rested, and already highly educated on the ways of the 4th RTB. With fresh legs, this was going to be a cakewalk.

But I quickly realized I was not, in fact, in for a cakewalk. As the day continued, my "well-rested" legs tightened. Although my feet felt better, they continued to look like tartare. My left shoulder had hated me since Malvesti, and my right knee had never stopped nagging me after getting sat on. I wasn't sure what was going on with my body, but it needed to stop. Time to "fake it till I make it." Getting and staying motivated was difficult, though. Being able to count down the days last time made it easier. This time, I crossed off the same numbers, one to twenty-one, and didn't feel like I was any closer to the finish line. Every day was frustrating.

The new guys thought they knew all about us women from reading the newspapers and hearing that we were Pieces of Shit (PoSs). I realized trying to build rapport with my male colleagues would actually be harder than the first time because I hadn't gone through RAP week with them. They hadn't seen me get smoked and keep pushing. They hadn't seen me fireman carry other students a gazillion times. They didn't know how hard I worked. They didn't know which rumors to believe. Add being a recycle to my already steep hill to climb, and I wasn't going to be able to let off the gas at all for the next two weeks. Plus, as a woman, I walked a narrow path. I couldn't be too friendly because somehow being friendly translated to wanting to have sex. I also couldn't be too much of an introvert because that translated to "She's a bitch."

My basic first impression of A-Co was that the cadre wanted to make everything much harder than required for some sort of sophomoric bragging rights. I was worried about getting my "Go." The standard here was different than B-Co's and also different from what we'd been taught by C-Co cadre during recycle. We also had more sensitive items to carry than we did in B-Co, including metal balls that were supposed to represent hand grenades. This squad also had one less man than my last squad but the same amount of gear to divide among us, so that extra equipment had more impact.

There were some great soldiers in my squad, but we also had some rocks. Morgan, the biggest guy in the squad, never volunteered to carry extra weight—or volunteered for anything, period. Dom talked a good game but was actually clueless. And Murray was just a dumbass.

But Charles was the worst. Charles was a military training instructor and an infantry NCO but had no aptitude for small-unit tactics. He couldn't hear worth shit. He couldn't navigate his way out of a paper bag. The Land Navigation course should have weeded his incompetent ass out. But his worst attribute was his nonstop complaining.

Ranger School was a team event. If any of these guys messed up, he could make those in other leadership billets fail as well. I could only pray they would have minimal impact on my chance at success.

THE FIRST TEST

We spent Day Ten learning about reconnaissance with an RI who actually liked instructing. I was assigned as squad leader for Actions-On the Objective during the mission (I was in charge during the actual execution of the recon mission). I was really excited because my only critiques thus far had been about how I wasn't as comfortable as I should be in the woods. This was an ungraded exercise, so I got some reps with immediate and honest feedback without negative repercussions. I was glad this exercise was ungraded because Charles was my ATL and Morgan was my BTL. Two equally clueless team leaders that tested both my leadership skills and resolve. I just prayed I didn't get stuck with these two clowns when it was my graded patrol. Neither of my team leaders understood the tactical steps required to complete a recon mission. I don't think they even wrote them down during our class. I had to let them use my Ranger Handbook during mission planning. My Handbook was tabbed and had additional notes in it. For some bizarre reason, my classmates enjoyed drawing male genitalia on anything and everything they could get their hands on, thus I rarely let the book leave my sight. Loaning out my Ranger Handbook was truly an act of kindness on my part.

During the mission, Charles was supposed to pull overwatch at one spot while Morgan and I maneuvered around the site to get eyes on the enemy position. As we low crawled up to his spot, Charles saw the "enemy," squawked, jumped to his feet, and just ran. Literally ran away while I lay there on the ground in the prone (laying as flat as possible on my stomach with my weapon oriented toward the enemy). I have no idea where he was going or why he would jump up when he saw the enemy. The point of a recon mission is to find and then observe in order to collect information. The event was both tragic and comical. I didn't know whether to cry, scream, or laugh.

Charles led the night movement to the exfiltration (or extraction, EXFIL) linkup heading back to Camp Darby. The EXFIL is how we tactically leave the site after mission completion. The RI was cool all day, but as Charles guided us in the completely wrong direction, followed a random path through the woods, and then forced us to wade through the deepest part of Hollis Creek during an ungraded patrol, the coolness faded. Eventually, even the RI had seen enough. He gave Charles a Major Minus for incompetence. Any hope I had had that this squad would be my ticket to Mountains faded.

HORRIBLE PATROL #1

It was May 22, the second day of graded patrols. So far, A-Co emplaced the exact same chain of command as they did during the original cadre-led/cadre-assisted training days. That put me on the hook for Actions-On the Objective as squad leader for a reconnaissance mission with the same leadership team as before. Unfortunately, that meant my ability to pass a patrol and move on to Mountains Phase walked hand in hand with the leadership abilities of the mouth-breathing Charles. I. WAS. SCREWED.

"Okay, Lisa—get it together. You know what you've got in him. He's just going to take more management and supervision. Not everybody is fire and forget." I tried pep talking myself. I glanced over at Charles, and I snorted at the absurdity of my task.

Charles kicked off the patrol by guiding us completely off course, even though I asked another, more competent soldier to help keep Charles on azimuth. Charles just ignored everything my buddy and I said when trying to get him back on course, and we ended up compromising another squad's area and mission. That is actually hard to do because Ranger School offsets the patrols by hundreds of meters.

I ended up firing Charles, which guaranteed he failed. I waited as long as I could and tried not to, but Charles just kept screwing up and wouldn't listen to anyone's guidance. I should have fired him earlier—like right as we stepped off on the patrol. I was 100 percent positive I'd failed my patrol. But I was determined to push through to the end of mission.

One of the worst and best parts of Ranger School was the team-work requirement. While being evaluated, your grade was part your actions but also part the actions of your teammates. Sometimes, that really works out well, and other times, not so much. I worked hard that day, even after I knew I'd failed, so hopefully we could still get Morgan a "Go" and set the rest of the squad up for an easy evening where they could get some rest and prepare for the next day.

*Directing a movement while squad leader
during training at Camp Darby.*

MORE NONSENSE FROM CHARLES

For the first day of our second field problem, Murray, a real win-
ner, was assigned as the BTL. The RIs gave us the chain of com-
mand the night prior so we could lean forward in the foxhole. I
had finally caught a break. Knowing the chain of command early
would greatly aid in the patrol planning and help us be more

organized...except Murray's dumbass went to sick call instead. Who the hell goes to sick call when he has a graded position?! Or, if injured, why wouldn't you tell the RI when you received your assignment so we could shift roles? It was especially bad because the BTL was responsible for gear distribution, test firing weapons, food and water, and a bunch of other stuff that all had to happen first thing in the morning for the group to succeed during the day. So basically, everything he was getting graded on he missed, and someone else had to complete. We each had to do our own work, and now we also had to cover his.

Charles was assigned as the planning bay squad leader. Since it was obvious Charles didn't know anything about planning or tactics, I wondered if this was the RI's way of making sure he didn't get a "Go." Or maybe they were testing the professionalism and the resolve of the rest of us.

A super whiny and uptight soldier ended up as the ATL. His pucker factor shot out the roof. He would NOT be getting a "Go" today with these two idiots in important roles. It was going to be entertaining. It made me a little happy that these clowns were getting their second looks now because it meant I wouldn't get stuck with them for my own second look. By my calculus, my chances of success just skyrocketed. The downside was having two incompetent team leaders and one highly stressed, low-functioning leader equated to a bad day ahead and, mostly likely, no sleep that night.

The WARNO and OPORD briefings were actually worse than I could have imagined. Not having a good plan and a worse briefing set everyone up for failure. The afternoon leadership was stuck with no information and a shitty plan, and the entire squad was tired and frustrated for the start of the Field Training Exercise (FTX). I was the Radio Telephone Operator (RTO), which meant my pack was really heavy and I had to run around the formation a lot. It also meant I wouldn't be called up for the second graded lineup. A squared-away leadership team allows the RTO to be an effective tool to communicate with adjacent units and higher headquarters. Incompetent leadership required me to cover down on the things they should have done for the sake of completing the mission. If I pushed myself hard enough, paid attention, and made up for their shortfalls, the afternoon leadership might have a chance at success. That was a very shaky "might," though. So I followed Charles around the planning bay and told him what to brief next. Our absent BTL just got a zero for everything in the morning while another student tried to cover for him. I received compliments as the RTO. It was a really rough, tiring morning for me as I ran around picking up the detritus the leaders had left in their wake. Their plan defined "shit show." We changed leadership early, probably because the RI could read the tea leaves as well as we all could, and we had a two-hour lightning stand-down immediately afterward. While running around earlier, I had sweat through my uniform. By the time the storm was in full swing, I was shivering. We dropped all our gear and found some low ground to sit in. Prior to stepping off, the RI told us to follow him. He moved us almost a full kilometer, saying our satellite imagery was wrong, which was a very nice way of making sure the morning's incompetence didn't hinder the afternoon leadership's success. Once we got around to executing the mission, it was a tad rushed, but I think the afternoon crowd got "Go"s.

SNAFU CENTRAL

The best explanation I heard about the inconsistencies in grading criteria was that if the RIs thought you would be an asset to the Ranger community, they would pass you unless you completely bolo'd (military slang for "failed") your patrol. The "High Ranger Standard" is an elusive thing. I got that, and I was okay with it. I knew people of different ranks were graded differently for sure. I also knew that branch mattered. The expectations were not the same for all in the military, nor should they be. But I wondered how the standard was applied to me.

Many of the Ris were coming around. Some of them never would, but at least it felt like they were no longer working against me. Unfortunately, I didn't think there was enough support to allow the female students to move on. The Ranger community was tight. Who wanted to risk their relationships and career to support a female Ranger?

As we rolled into Day Seventeen, the RI had the second leadership team set up the patrol base, which was different than usual. It was the wee hours of the morning, and our normal routine was for the next morning's first leadership to set it up. I think he wanted to give the guys he was grading a few more opportunities to succeed so they could get their "Go"s. He gave us two hours and extremely specific instructions on what to do. He had given us a really thorough class that morning on his expectations when he came on as our RI. Between his morning instruction and his end-of night-guidance, our patrol base looked amazing.

Right before bed, the RI announced the new chain of command. For my second and final look, I was assigned ATL, which put me in charge of land nav. Land nav was my thing! This was going to go so smooth! I knew my shit. All I had to do was make sure the sand table was good and lead these guys through the woods. We would appropriately react to contact when I spotted the enemy. Too easy. This was my last opportunity to get a "Go." If I failed this one, I'd be on the first thing smoking back to Texas.

But then the RI put Murray, the guy who went to sick call during his last leadership role, as squad leader, and Charles as BTL. The same Charles that I had to fire during a graded patrol previously. Holy crappy leadership team. However, as the ATL, I didn't need the squad leader or BTL to be proficient for me to pass. I just had to worry about my lane. I could do this. The RIs talked, so they knew how bad a situation they were putting me in. I couldn't control the card I got dealt, but I got a vote on how I played it.

Before he left for the day, the RI told me to make sure my terrain model was spot on and paragraph 1 of the Fragmentary Order (FRAGO) was perfect, and I would be golden. I got the feeling that in his mind, I was ready to move on to Mountains Phase.

The next morning, our new RI showed up at 0630, and the first thing he did was move our patrol base. That meant we had to redo everything. My beautiful terrain model was destroyed with a few kicks, and I would have to build another one from scratch. Then he told me there was a "screw up" and I was actually supposed to be the squad leader. He moved Murray to ATL and kept Charles as BTL. The other roles stayed the same. Somehow, they had only screwed up my assignment. To top it all off, SFC Hazemore appeared as our walker (grader) for the day. Fuck! He hated women, especially me. Serenity prayer.

On the surface, the patrol base looked okay, but it got pretty bad once the RI started digging deeper. Emplacing a claymore mine is a basic soldier task. The actual mine has the words "front toward enemy" stamped on the business side. While playing catch up from the RI's "screw up," I didn't make time to spot check all the claymores Charles emplaced. I incorrectly assumed a promotable infantry staff sergeant, whose duty description included leading an infantry squad and who was getting graded on patrol-base security, could handle properly covering dead space with claymores. I was so very wrong. He chose completely useless locations. In addition, our sectors of fire, also his job, were not interlocking between positions. This was also a basic soldier task. I should have checked, but since my two team leaders were incapable of doing anything on their own, they were not able to help with the FRAGO, and I had to do it 100 percent by myself. "Trust but verify" was a great motto...if you have more than an hour and just yourself to do three hours' and peoples' worth of work.

As squad leader, I got docked for all their mistakes.

By mid-morning, things were so screwed up I had to change priorities of work for the squad. We started fixing the patrol base when we really needed to be prepping for the day's mission.

We were attacked by the OP4 while eating chow and disseminating information about the mission. I could only describe the morning with the acronym SNAFU—Situation Normal: All Fucked Up.

When we were loading trucks to get to our infiltration (INFIL) point, the squad was slow to get their rucks on, causing us to get hit by indirect fire. Everyone was tired and moving like pond water. Murray didn't get down on the ground once the artillery simulators started. In fact, he didn't bother to even so much as duck, so the RI made him a casualty. Our casualty evacuation (CASEVAC) plan was for the ATL (Murray) to manage security while the BTL (Charles) managed casualties. Although the CASEVAC plan hadn't changed since we started working as a squad days before, AND I had the team leaders back brief it during the FRAGO, they still screwed it up! Somehow, the exact plan and system that had worked flawlessly for the past five days failed miserably today—the only difference was the leadership.

Once SFC Hazemore realized he killed my ATL, he switched the casualty from Murray to someone else in the squad and made it merely an arm injury. We had to move quickly to get out of the kill zone. Murray finally got moving. Since he was supposed to be leading our formation, no one could go before he did. Once he started moving, he was really moving—way too quickly, considering we had a casualty. I reminded the BTL, Charles, that he was responsible for our injured soldier and to "make sure we maintain 100 percent accountability of the squad," as that was his job. I knew he wouldn't do it, but I made sure Hazemore heard me tell Charles. I hoped that, somehow, I would be forgiven for the inevitable fuck up that Charles would produce. Charles then tried physically lifting our casualty into a fireman carry, even though it was a fucking injured arm. I could not make this shit up if I tried.

We finally got everyone moving, with our M240 gun in trail. The M240 said they were the last to leave the security halt, but I couldn't find Charles. I sent the RTO to the front to stop the rest of the squad. We had moved less than one hundred meters in fucking daylight. My graded patrol would be over as soon as we made it out of this clearing. We just had to hold it together for a little longer. Once I called a halt, I heard Charles yelling, "A1-2, A1-2!" That was our squad call sign. My heart sank. He wasn't more than thirty meters from me. If you got lost or separated from the group, you were supposed to call out the squad call sign to make sure you didn't get left behind. At some point, Charles had turned himself around while walking through ten meters of thickish brush. He couldn't see or hear anybody, so he panicked. Had he just walked straight, he would have run right into the rest of the squad. It was official: as soon as Charles yelled that, he, the casualty, and the two ruck bearers were "lost" from the squad formation; I automatically failed my patrol.

The saddest part of this comical episode was they were "lost" while still in the middle of the squad. Our lead and trail elements remained intact. We trained Stop, Look, Listen, Smell (SLLS) constantly while conducting movements. He was so close to the rest of the squad that if he had stopped and listened, he would have heard others moving through the brush. Well, maybe not his deaf ass. Even more amusing, had he stopped, the M240 team would have physically bumped right into him. He was close enough he probably could have smelled the rest of us. It was a short movement during daylight in mild terrain. That was my easiest and worst Darby patrol.

Sadly, I don't even know how I could have avoided the problems. I was furious the RIs had assigned me the same guy I had fired during my last patrol. Then, I was mad at Charles. Then, I was mad at myself for wasting time trying to teach that bumbling idiot. It was over. Right then and there, my dream of a Ranger Tab died.

Everyone knew that short of holding Charles's hand, I could not have done anything more to keep him in line with the rest of the squad. He was a casualty of Ranger School, but sometimes, when that grenade goes off, it has ancillary consequences. I was an unintended casualty—or maybe not. Maybe Charles was the cannon fodder, and I was the target. Either way, GAME OVER. That was my last chance. I would go home without my tab while everyone else went to Mountains together. When the night movement started and everything was dark, I let myself cry for about ten seconds. I had given it everything and come up short.

The guys in my platoon were all saying they heard about how I got screwed in both my patrols. Knowing my classmates thought I got a raw deal helped my fragile ego. During downtime, a young LT randomly approached me and shook my hand. He said he was impressed and honored to know me. He told me he really thought he would hate being in Ranger School with women. Then he just walked away. It was a good reminder I may have demons to slay and things to prove, but so did these guys. They had to be adult enough to keep an open mind, allowing those of us here to change their opinions of women in the military. It was guys like that who would ultimately argue with their friends about us and maybe lose some buddies over it. These young soldiers discovered we merely wanted the same opportunities they had. Seeing is believing.

Murray and Charles recycled. The other eleven guys in my squad were moving on. That was a phenomenal pass rate, especially in comparison to Class 6-15. I was overjoyed for all of them. Each thanked me individually for helping them succeed. Later, a guy from the SNAFU squad recycled back into my platoon. He said the squad absolutely fell apart in Mountains, and they blamed it on losing me. That made me sad. I loved those guys. But it also gave me an ego stroke that I added value to my team.

GO HOME OR KEEP GOING

None of the eight female students had passed any of their patrols. The second I heard that, I knew the school had decided our fate long before I ever shaved my head. Ranger School was not ready for strong, competent women.

I was furious no female students had passed. Historical stats suggest if you make it past RAP week, which eight of us did, then 75 percent should graduate.[9] The women sent to this school were more closely scrutinized prior to leaving their units than any male

---

9   Airborne and Ranger Training Brigade, "ARTB Course Information."

soldier had ever been, which should mean we could expect a higher percentage of graduates. We each attended and passed RTAC prior to coming. How could every single female soldier at Ranger School be that tactically incompetent? Each female hopeful had two to three patrols per Darby attempts. That meant in over forty tries, not one of us could get a single "Go," while medics and mechanics with two to three years in the army did. Bullshit.

Even some of the RIs could admit we were getting a raw deal. One of the RIs pulled me aside to let me know I needed to come back and be the first female graduate if they ever actually opened Ranger School to women. He told me I was exactly the type of soldier who should be wearing the tab.

Although painfully disappointed, I admit I was excited to get home. Who knew how I would feel once the dust settled, but right then, I knew escaping that toxic environment was exactly what I needed. I could also admit, without a doubt, that I failed my Class 7-15 patrols. I knew it with the same certainty I knew I should have passed my Class 6-15 patrols, at least one of them.

On my nineteenth, and final, day as a member of Class 7-15, we woke up at 0400 for an early MRE and then were off to our Brigade Boards. The Brigade Commander was the last person who had to tell us we failed before we were officially dropped from the course. Once that was done, we would start out-processing immediately. The Army made everything excruciatingly painful, and my departure from Ranger School was no exception. All the failures sat around for a bit. The mood was grim, and everyone talked about how they got screwed. We chatted and bitched, mostly bitched.

While waiting for our boards, an RI brought some mail. All the love, support, and encouragement I received was amazing and made me feel like I had let family, friends, and complete strangers down. In order to counterbalance the impending depression and self-deprecation, I kept refining my plans to return to normal. Life goes on, and self-pity never got me anywhere. Ultimately, I decided I needed to start my personal fitness program back up immediately. Like, right now! While waiting to talk to the colonel, I did set after set of push-ups, air-squats, and good-mornings. It was wonderful catharsis. I smoked myself, and it felt good working out my frustrations. Done with Ranger School, and back to CrossFit, Oly Lifting, and Brazilian Jiu Jitsu. Back to my career, and, most importantly, back to my family. I had stepped into the arena when I had the chance. I had failed honorably and could hold my head high.

I was the last person to see the Brigade Commander. I reported in, still sweat soaked from my self-imposed PT session, and stood at the position of attention. I knew there would be a discussion, as many eyes were on this man. I told him I knew where I messed up. I owned my failures. But now wasn't the time to hold back, so I also told him about the piss-poor team leaders I had for both my missions. I cited the fact that one of my bumbling, idiot team leaders was the same for both graded patrols. I also mentioned I was changed from ATL to squad leader the morning of the mission.

I sensed we were wrapping this little chat up. I took a big breath and got borderline belligerent. For some reason, I didn't mind getting dropped from the school, but it bothered me I had failed in something I had mastery in. "Sir, I don't want to leave Ranger School and read in the newspapers I couldn't figure out tactics. That's bullshit. When you're done with me, go read what my peers said about my tactics. Sir, this shit is easy."

"Jaster, if you can do forty-nine perfect RANGER push-ups right now, I'll give you a Day One restart." He pointed to the space on his office floor between my feet and his desk. Oh shit. I had literally spent the last thirty minutes thrashing myself, and now I had to do push-ups. I never blinked. I got right down and started pushing. My arms were screaming when I hit twenty. I held plank for great amounts of time between reps, but I painfully pushed my body away from the earth forty-nine ugly times. I got up. Yeah, I got forty-nine, but even the kindest RI would have a hard time calling those "perfect" by any standard.

"That doesn't really give me confidence you are physically ready for a Day One, Jaster."

I didn't say anything. I just stood there staring at him in silence wondering what in the hell I had just done.

After what seemed like an eternity, an RI in the back of the colonel's office piped up. "Sir, I just watched Ranger Jaster outside for the better part of an hour PTing the shit out of herself. That's probably why she looked like ass."

That was just enough. The colonel nodded in acknowledgment. "Okay. Day One restart if you want it, Jaster."

Nope. No, I do not. With all my heart, I do not want that. I'm ready to go home to my wonderful life. My brain wasn't listening to my heart, and my mouth said, "Hell yes, sir! I can do this!" I remembered that every single second at this school was truly an opportunity of a lifetime.

That phone call with Big Al (Allan, my husband) was hard. "Hey, Lisa, we knew this wasn't going to be easy, but we're not talking about easy or hard. I'm all about a Day One restart, but you gotta give me something. I need to believe you're gonna get a fair shake." I couldn't give him the assurance he wanted. But I had to stay. "Okay. Okay. Fucking give 'em hell, baby. I love you." We hung up.

I had redefined success. At first, it was earning that Ranger Tab. Then, as that moved out of reach, the goal became changing the minds of the hundreds of young men I teamed with in that school. All those young soldiers would reenter the army ranks expecting more from the female soldiers they worked with. The change in attitude of the RIs, as well as the young men who were my classmates, would slowly trickle into the army. I got to watch while one by one, as those guys got to know me or another female soldier, they would indicate a change of heart in the most subtle ways. It was cute, like dating in seventh grade. They might give you some Skittles or swap peanut butter with you. They might hand you your ruck instead of throwing it down a few feet away when grabbing gear. Each young officer or enlisted man with whom I struggled through Ranger School now understood that being a female soldier didn't matter—being a good soldier did.

CHAPTER 6

DOUBTS

Day 1 Recycle

May 31–June 21

My depression about being sent home had turned into excitement about moving forward with the rest of my life, and then back on the merry-go-round heading into depression again. Day One meant RAP week again. It meant another twelve-mile hike and five-mile run. I had to redo all the shit I had already done just to get to patrols.

It didn't take long before I started questioning my decision. "What have I done?" I was not sure I could make it through another RAP week after all this time away from training. I had definitely lost muscle mass and cardiovascular fitness. Patrols all day and night, sleep deprivation, and starvation don't prepare the body for the rigors of RAP week. I had serious work to do.

The physical aspect was huge, but there was a looming second issue too. There would be a three-week hold in Vaughan's Platoon while I waited to restart. That meant I would start with Class 8-15 the day AFTER I was supposed to graduate. Was I mentally tough enough to handle that with professionalism and grace? I would have lots of time to ponder all the important stuff I was missing, from Zac's birthday to critical events at work, to being there for my husband while he was in battalion command.

I couldn't stay here another month just to fail.

THE ATHENA 3

Three women and several men were invited to start over. All three women said, "Yes," and the men all declined. I'm not mad at the guys who said, "No, thanks." Being offered a "Day One restart" is akin to throwing a drowning person an anvil.

So it was down to Shaye Haver, Kristen Griest, and me. I dubbed us the "Athena 3." Coming into our restart, I barely knew them. But now, we did everything together and quickly got close. I didn't have a lot of people, other than Allan and my family, that were full-time friends. Most people only knew a version of me—the nerd, the current-events junky, the gym rat, etc. These ladies were cut from the same cloth, so they understood ALL of me.

I felt like the big sister. I wanted to shelter and protect them from so many things, even though they were the most competent women I had ever met. I told too many stories about Allan. I wanted them to know men exist that truly love and support strong women while remaining strong themselves. I wanted to show that although it was hard to have two driven people in one family, it was possible. It was also okay to find that loving, supportive partner that wasn't driven and would rather raise you up while sitting in the shadows. But that needed to be a conscious decision before walking down the aisle.

We were the only three Day Ones, which soon became our title. "Day Ones!!!" could be heard being bellowed throughout Camp Rogers frequently. The rest of the recycles would not have to go through RAP week again. We would.

Early during our time in Vaughan's Platoon, the First Sergeant (1SG) pulled the Day Ones aside to check on our status. The fact that there were only three of us increased our visibility, and any incident involving us would incite a media shitstorm. During our conversation, he also asked how the barracks situation was working for us. We let him know that having three people on one side and fifty-seven on the other was unfair, especially when seven of them were sleeping on cots rather than beds.

After our candid discussion, 1SG lightened the segregation regulations. Thank God! Integration through segregation never worked and never would. We set up the barracks so we could sleep separated but otherwise combined with the guys. We blocked off one end by opening a couple locker doors, giving us complete visual privacy. When we were not changing, we closed the doors. We weren't ostracized, and the guys weren't mad at us for them having to sleep on cots.

Athena 3 was here, and we weren't broken.

DAILY LIFE AS A RECYCLE

I wasn't sure how to count the days anymore. May 31 was my first day as a recycle. But I was also on my seventh week at a nine-week school. And I had three weeks until I even "started." You know you're not doing well when tracking your progress gets that complicated.

Our daily schedule was light and easy and quiet. Everyone met up for a breakfast MRE. We had a class, ate an MRE for lunch, did some PEs, and then ate another MRE for dinner. Many days, we'd go on a work detail. Sometimes, we'd have a religious service provided by a fellow recycle who was a chaplain. Kris, Shaye, and I flew low and did our work details as professionals, but all three of us had a laser focus on healing and preparing for the grueling RAP week we were facing once again. For me, the RPFT would again be a challenge, except this time, I'd be run down from weeks of eating shit food and wouldn't have the benefit of a specific training regimen.

This recycle was different than the last. No one looked at their Ranger Handbooks while waiting in line for chow. Since Camp Rogers was basically closed down, we rarely ran from one location to another and talked openly with the other students. Some kept a Bible in their pockets, but no one was utilizing static time for "opportunity training."

I have always filled my time with productive effort. If I watch TV, I stretch or fold laundry. If I read a lot of emails, I do so on a stationary bike. I tried to squeeze as much as I could out of each day. Keeping with my personality, I wrote in my journals while we were standing in line and often got unsolicited input from those around me. I thought I would get picked on, but the other students, and even some of the RIs, continually pushed me to capture the experience.

As Kris, Shaye, and I became more and more normalized in everyone's eyes, some even started messing with me, asking if they could choose their own pseudonyms in my book.

"Write a book? This is Ranger School, not BUD/S [Navy SEAL training]," I would joke.

Somehow, me journaling turned into "Jaster is writing a book," and that turned into "What can my name be, Jaster?" and "Who will play me in the movie version?" The support was odd because I didn't understand life the way they did. I still believed I was just another Ranger Student trying to get my tab.

Since we had three weeks in this crazy limbo and I needed to be at peak condition at the end of it, I decided to finally admit a weakness and seek help for a nagging physical condition. One of my peers was a medic at Fort Bragg, and since my hip was killing me, I thought I would bug him about it. I couldn't go to sick call until Monday, and maybe he could give me a diagnosis, allowing me to avoid the extra attention all together. He thought I had strained my psoas. His advice was to rest for two weeks to heal, take NSAIDs, and use lots of ice. Well, that was useless advice. If his assessment was correct, I was screwed for RAP week. Hopefully, adding excessive amounts of prayer could replace the medical protocol prescribed by the medic.

I tried to do some push-ups, crunches, and chin-ups, but all three actions engage my core and therefore hurt. I was limping pretty badly. A classmate gave me some of his Naproxen and Tylenol, which would hold me over until sick call, as long as I didn't get caught with it. The medics handed it out like candy, so the RIs knew everyone in the barracks had it, but I didn't want anyone making an example of me.

First Sergeant told me I needed to sham (pretend to push while really taking it easy) for the next week because no one gets sent home for physically failing in Vaughan's Platoon, but they do get sent home for physically falling apart during RAP week. He said I better improve myself physically because he had $20 riding on me making it all the way to Victory Pond (the graduation site). He said he couldn't afford to lose $20, so if I made him into a liar, I would owe him big. The fact that his confidence in me only garnered a $20 wager pissed me off. But the point was made: the tides of the institution were slowly shifting.

I believed the three primary Vaughan's Platoon NCOs truly wanted to see us succeed. Staff Sergeant Worthy said he wanted to see us pass to make people shut the hell up. His story was a good one. He joined the Army late and went to Ranger School when he was thirty-six. He was tough as hell during his prime but had since severely damaged his knees and back, like most infantry NCOs. He worked his body hard and never recovered or took care of it. Now, he was overweight and couldn't do much physically. In most units, people would have understood, but as an RI at Ranger School, the students and other cadre judged him. They assumed he wasn't capable because he had lost his fitness or that he had never done anything in the past because he was fat now. He had his war stories. He did the job of an infantryman by closing with and destroying the enemy—up close and personal. I had judged him. And now, as he drew the parallel between people judging him unfairly and people judging us, I grew up a little.

MISSING MY FAMILY

Motivation was difficult, but reminders of what I gave up to be here helped.

I hung a picture of Zac and Tori in my locker during this recycle. Tori was wearing a Wonder Woman shirt that I bought her to match a Wonder Woman sports bra I had. It had a cape—the shirt, not the bra. Zac was wearing a Batman T-shirt with matching Batman socks. The socks had little capes as well. They were my little superheroes. Seeing their faces every day made me both sad and happy simultaneously.

I knew telling my little ones they have to be part of the solution, they need to put themselves out there, and they are built to do something great meant I needed to set the example. But I hated missing the daily drop-offs at school and the goodnight cuddles. Nine weeks away, or twelve at the most, had seemed like an easy stretch. It was nothing compared to deployments and what thousands of soldiers sacrifice every day. I was at a school, a voluntary school I could leave at any time. I had no right to complain. But it was going to be eighteen weeks at least without kisses and hugs. Especially since all passes except the Saturday before insertion had been canceled to ensure the class stayed focused on training. Since we had been told we'd get passes every Saturday, everyone was crushed. My dumbass had let the idea of seeing my husband the following weekend set in. Fuck this stupidity.

The worst part of this little change of plans was that the guys blamed the women. The previous precedent was Saturday AND Sunday passes. They thought having us here brought too much attention to the school, and we were all on lockdown to ensure media didn't find out who was left.

When I called Allan to tell him about the change of plans, it was difficult. Earlier, he had seemed doubtful that trying to pass Darby on my third attempt would bring a different result, no matter what I did. Now, I heard his spirit start to break over the phone for the first time. Apparently, he had had great expectations for the visit as well. He composed himself quickly, but there was a definite waver.

What am I doing? Seriously, this was never a goal of mine. I wasn't brooding at West Point, angry because I couldn't branch infantry. I never pined about going to Ranger School when I was an LT. Hell, I am not even active duty anymore!!!!

Since we were only allowed to use the phones on weekends, I wrote Zac and Tori every day. I missed them so much and wished I could see them on my one pass day. I know some of the dads here felt the same way. Unfortunately for the guys, showing a desire to be with their families was a sign of weakness. I guess that was one aspect that was easier for me. Women were expected to be more emotional than men; therefore, I was authorized to miss my family.

I had worried so much before I left about how my absence would impact my loved ones, I had forgotten to come to grips with how it might impact me. Tori learned how to ride a bike while I was gone, so Allan bought her a new, pink bike. I had promised to do that with her. It made me really sad that I missed the opportunity to teach my daughter how to ride a bike. My family was thriving; they didn't "need" me and found ways to maintain a normal balance with only one parent. That made it a bit easier to be here, but it was also really hard realizing I had written myself out of this chapter of my kids' lives.

Missing my kiddos was one thing. What was really hurting my soul right now, though, was not being able to talk to my partner, my best friend. That was hell on earth. I needed his reassurance and confidence.

To make the news from home even worse, Allan told me during one of our few phone calls that Shell was eliminating my position. I had until the end of September to post for a new job in the company. If I didn't find one, I would receive a severance package. I didn't think they could do that while I was out on military training, but I wasn't certain. If the whole department went away, they might just be able to let me go. I volunteered for this school, so that might also change the laws that applied to my service. With no internet access, there was nothing I could do.

When I would call my family, the worst part was always saying goodbye. I could hear my babies still yelling updates into the phone. They wanted to share with me, and I was hanging up. My heart broke every call home.

My children were without a mother, my husband was without a partner, my hip was injured, my professional career was going to shit, and I had been gone for eight weeks...and I hadn't even started Ranger School yet. This was starting to feel like a bad investment. My situation was becoming a case study in sunk costs. *Please, God, let this amount to something, or I will have thrown away too much.*

EMOTIONAL ROLLERCOASTER

I thought to myself, *I will succeed at RAP Week: Part Two, no matter what. If we make this go around without any of the three of us being dropped, the physical strength argument will be permanently squashed. That alone is reason to push. Based on the male success rates after being a Day One restart, we have a high hill to climb, but I completed RAP week once before, I will do it again.*

I was so incredibly sick of trying to see the positive side of everything. When you start to feel like you're a pawn in a bigger game, it really fucks with your head. I felt like quitting. Hell, even if they did let us move onto Mountains, how long would they make me stay there? If I made it through Darby and on to Mountains, I was certain I would recycle there. I knew that was a bad attitude to have, but it made sense. All three of us couldn't go straight through after all three of us recycled the first phase three times. It would look bad for the school. I fully expected to do Mountains twice and then get dropped. "Reserve mother of two tried hard but just couldn't make it," was an easy sell. I don't really fit the "Ranger community" demographic and couldn't imagine being "allowed" to wear the tab.

I would make bets with myself. *Jaster, if you can do this run under time, you won't quit. Jaster, if you can do this ruck march, you won't quit.*

My quitting side lost every bet. I was lying to myself the whole time. There wasn't an ounce of quit in me. I have only ever really quit something once, an Exterra Race, and I still regret it. What would the next eleven weeks be compared to earning that tab in the big scheme of things? As long as my kids forgave me for leaving them, this would all be worth it. I just had to keep reminding myself that although I was separated from those I loved, this was a one-time deal that could positively impact a lot of policies and lives, not just ours. Nothing worth doing was easy, right?

In an attempt to do something worthwhile during my three-week recycle, I took my memo notepad that I wrote in every day and started writing a journal I could send home to my family. I hoped to capture everything that happened the first seven weeks before I forgot the details. Each day I had been in Georgia, I wrote out mission information, chain of command, and other critical data. I also took a few notes on personalities and events, knowing someday I would be faced with explaining my absence to my children. I wanted them to know why I was doing this and understand the internal conflict I faced every day I was away from them. As I started putting my notes together in coherent thoughts and stories, a rush of emotion filled me. Writing everything out convinced me I was staying for the right reasons. Somehow, writing things down helped me sort out all that was going on around me. This was not just about being the first or doing something no one else had done. It was about proving to myself and anyone who cared to look in my direction that I was no less competent than my fellow engineer officers just because I was a woman.

CLASS 6-15 GRADUATES

Day Seventeen of the three-week recycle was another emotional rollercoaster. My hip hurt, and I was thoroughly annoyed with some of the students. The small spaces, frustrating conditions, contrasting experiences, differing ranks, and varying maturity levels were getting to all of us. After lunch, I was able to check my email due to all my work issues. While online, I discovered Shell was not paying my full salary because I was on military duty, and the Army wasn't paying me at all. I had been there almost two straight months without getting paid. One more kick in the shins with regard to this experience. To add insult to an already injured spirit, Class 6-15, my original Ranger Class, had returned from Swamps to prep for graduation.

I was supposed to restart in seven days. I was nervous as hell, but I needed to move closer to the end of this adventure than the beginning. I started thinking there was a chance they would let us get a tab. I was sad my internal conversations didn't center around "me being good enough;" it was all still, "Will they *let* me?" "Let" was out of my control. I couldn't control what my grader thought about me invading his fraternity, and I had no tools to fix it.

That being said, the tone around me shifted during that recycle. The RIs seemed to gradually come around. The scowls started to fade a little. Maybe the RIs needed some time to come to terms with the idea of female Rangers. Maybe some of the original nineteen women were not up to the task, and I got lumped in with them. Maybe after watching us, they had sorted through their cognitive dissonance and reconciled that there are some women who can do this. Allan validated my suspicions when he told me about a news report where a camera crew asked an RI, "What is the difference between the male and female Ranger students?" The RI responded curtly with, "The women don't complain, they just work."

Prior to Class 6-15's graduation, I ate breakfast with four "old Rangers" who came in for the ceremony. They were going to speak with Class 6-15 during their rehearsal that day, and they seemed incredibly supportive of me being in the course. Funny how the old guys didn't seem threatened by the women here. They were Vietnam era and earlier. One of them said Ranger School is merely a test of mind + heart + gut. He was right. Nothing had changed.

CHAPTER 7

PASSING THE BRO TEST, ONE SOLDIER AT A TIME

Darby 3

Day 1–Day 14 / June 22–July 10

"I seen an old lady walkin' down the street

She had ropes in her hand, jungle boots on her feet.

I said, 'Hey, old lady, where you goin' to?'

She said, 'US Army Ranger School.'

I said, 'Hey, old lady, don't you think you're too old?

'Ranger School is for the young and the bold.'

She said, 'Hey, young punk, who you talkin' to?

'I'm an instructor at the Ranger School.'"

—My twist on "Seen an Old Lady"

It was the first day of my final chapter at Benning, no matter what. The Athena 3 had to be packed by 0700 for Day Zero insert. It was time to restart the madness. We put our "motivation masks" back on and headed out. We could feel sorry for ourselves when it was over.

The first major task of the day was to sit in a large room and listen to a few key people talk prior to starting in processing. This class was slightly smaller than the last two because the Georgia heat took the difficulty of Ranger School to a whole new level. It was fun listening to the speeches about quitting and giving up. The military does an excellent job of either firing people up or sucking their souls dry of all motivation during these types of speeches. This one was about my new favorite topic: quitting.

I contemplated, *Why would I ever want to quit? Probably loneliness for my family.* Then I asked myself, *What would my family think if I came home because I quit? They would be embarrassed.* When Allan left for Airborne School, my parting words to him were, "Don't come home without your wings." We both knew I wasn't completely kidding. He hadn't mastered the Parachute Landing Fall (PLF) and suffered a horrendous landing during tower week. Like a good marine, he hid the injury. His knee was so damaged he needed surgery as soon as he got home. But he *did* come home with his jump wings.

One of my biggest challenges while meeting the new class was answering the question, "So, what's your issue passing patrols?" I really wanted to reply, "The fact that I have four instead of five appendages," but that wouldn't help me. So I hid my bitterness and said as little as possible. It was hard to keep quiet because I couldn't have these guys thinking I was tactically incompetent; at the same time, I didn't need them thinking I couldn't take responsibility for my actions.

So why was I still here after nine weeks? Little girls like my Tori needed someone to look up to. Zac needed to understand how important it is to push yourself through challenges. Both my kids deserved a mother who saw things through to the end and set the example. They needed to know adjectives didn't decide my fate. I needed to get my tab to make all this time away from my family, plus all my training time before I left, worth it for them. So when the commanders gave speeches asking about quitters, all I heard were all the reasons to stay. Too many to count.

RAP WEEK...AGAIN

On Day Zero, we were released for bed at 2200, up at 0155, and formed up by 0215. Apparently, formation was at 0221, not 0220 or 0225; funny, RI. We headed over at 0230 but didn't get our brief until 0300. We started the RPFT at 0350. I got a total of one push-up cut and finished the run in 38:32. That was one minute and eighteen seconds faster than my April five-miler time. All the work I had put in during the previous three weeks trying to both heal and regain fitness paid off. I focused on the quarter-mile markers along the route rather than the pull in my right hip. It wasn't bad, but I still had a ways to go before I could run comfortably. Thankfully, the rest of the running at Ranger School wasn't graded.

My right hip was a little sore after the run and sit-ups, and my right knee still felt as bad as it did after the knife-pit sitting incident in April. Whatever I did to it was permanent. So far though, we hadn't had any real smoke sessions. I heard it was because the heat index was well over one hundred degrees each day, and the humidity was just shy of raining. The RIs couldn't make us do sets of more than ten reps of any one exercise for fear of breaking people off in the heat. I could actually use good form with sets that small without getting fatigued. I kept waiting for the yelling to start, for the RIs from Class 6-15 and Class 7-15 to pop out from behind this new Class 8-15 team.

Without getting smoked, this group wasn't really being held accountable for meeting timelines and working together to accomplish simple tasks. The class hadn't learned the importance of teamwork yet. A classmate who had been dropped after two attempts at Mountains the previous year stated the only way to get alpha males (the students) to respect other alpha males (the RIs) was through pure brute force and punishment. His point was they needed to "get fucked up" to learn respect. From what I saw, I agreed. You could also learn a lot from watching how the RIs treated the students during those random PT sessions. Whom do they hone in on? Are they especially attentive to those who don't look the part of a "Ranger?" Do they pay more attention to the guys not doing the exercises correctly? Are they creative with their physical punishments? Do they have a reason for making us do exercises? Do they change up the exercises, essentially making it a bit easier?

We ate an MRE pretty early and then headed down to the CWSA course. This time, we didn't run. That run had literally been the absolute worst part of RAP week for me the last time— sprinting to the CWSA site wearing boots and a full uniform while carrying all my gear in a trash bag. We walked a route that was much shorter than the way we had gone last time. We stayed on a wooded trail with lots of shade and walked painfully slow. Even then, people were feeling dizzy. I felt bad for the guys from cold climates. I had been there for months and was from Houston. I had trained for and ran an Ironman in this weather a couple years earlier, so walking in the shade was easy for me, despite the heat.

Since I had chipped my tooth in April on the zipline, I adjusted how my body addressed the water, landing by leaning WAY back this time when I needed to release the handles. I ended up skipping like a flat rock across the water. One of my RIs from RTAC was in charge of the station. I asked him cheerfully if he saw me skipping. He quickly scolded me about my professionalism. Then he lost all military bearing himself and roared with laughter. I am certain that would have made it onto *America's Funniest Home Videos*—or possibly *US Army WTF! Moments*.

I expected the cadre to make up for the lack of smoke sessions during our evening run on Malvesti. But as the day drew on, the RIs seem incredibly concerned about the temperature, reminding people there was no retribution for bringing up symptoms of heat-related injuries.

Because the RIs were so worried about the heat, the Darby Mile and Malvesti course were SO MUCH EASIER than during Class 6-15, but my Ranger Buddy was terrible. He was a foreign officer and a total waste of camouflage. He was completely devoid of ability and lacked motivation, resulting in additional attention in the pit. He couldn't do any of the obstacles, including simply holding himself up on the chin-up bar. He flat out refused to do some of the exercises, which of course meant I had to keep restarting them until he would complete the dictated set.

Then he needed to see a medic because he got something in his eye, which I totally understood, but I had to stay in the pit while he visited with the medic. SFC Hazemore and SFC Red took the opportunity to inflict as much pain as possible on me while I waited for my Ranger Buddy to rejoin me in the pit. I did jumping lunges and jumping Y-squats for most of the time he was gone. Did I mention that both of these RIs were around during our recycle? They knew my hip was an issue. And both of them told me I was starting to limp and needed to head to see the medic myself. I continued to respectfully decline their suggestions to walk out of the pit. SFC Hazemore accused me of disobeying a direct order. Two out-of-shape RIs who didn't live the creed they preached would not create any dents in my armor.

It may sound sick, but other than the fact that my legs turned into complete putty, getting smoked like that motivated the hell out of me. I felt like I was back in real Ranger School. It was comfortable. I was singled out in so many ways, but my responses were growing louder, and my jumps were getting higher. *Find a weaker soul to crush!*

The final barrier to getting into the heart of the course was the Day Four ruck march. I started this march with a plan. I was going to run all the downhills, of course, and all the flats. This time, I knew the course, so I knew I would need to get to four and a half miles well under my fifteen-minutes-per-mile mandatory split time to finish comfortably. Once we were rucking and started to spread out, there were two guys who walked until I ran. I would pass them, they would see it was me, then they would start sprinting to get ahead of me again. Over and over, we did this for much of the twelve-mile hike. One of them told me when we got to the finish line, he just couldn't let me beat him. The other one crossed the finish line a few yards in front of me and promptly was a heat casualty. The medics cooled him off and dropped him from the course. I felt sorry for the guy. My success shouldn't define him. But this was neither the first nor the last time someone lost focus by falling into my gameplan instead of keeping to their own.

My strategy had worked. With the exception of the two soldiers killing themselves to beat me, it was twelve completely uneventful miles done. No praying for strength, no chanting about my damn haircut, no bleeding feet, no desire to dump my water. Just one foot in front of the other for twelve long miles. I hit the six-mile turnaround at 1:24, which was nine minutes faster than last time. I think Kris finished second on the ruck, and I was tenth to fifteenth. We were both back on the rocks well ahead of the main mass of students. That made me feel good, especially because I knew I could have gone faster if I needed to. Not much faster, but I didn't go to dark places this time. One of the guys in my company said I was a beast, and he officially apologized for every ridiculous "Joe" thing he ever said about women, women in combat, and women in Ranger School. It was a pretty surreal moment for both of us. A reckoning. This, this right here, was why I had to stay. But I couldn't wait until they started assuming we were normal soldiers who just wanted to get out of this hellhole as fast as possible with our tabs, just like them.

JUMP DAY

June 27 was Jump Day. During my first attempt at Darby, the airborne operations were canceled due to high winds. For my second attempt, it was perfect skies and a smooth landing. This time, my third attempt to pass patrols at Camp Darby felt surreal for some reason. It was cool and a little cloudy. Perfect jump weather. I was so excited to start again. I slept a little while we were flying, but some of the guys said I looked nervous. I must just always look that way based on the comments I kept hearing. It should have been an easy jump, except I had a bad exit. My mind was incredibly busy—and not in a good way. My risers twisted something fierce, and I struggled to stay focused on the event. Once I was flying straight and brushed off the mental cobwebs, I fixed my risers and looked to the horizon, as always. Every jump ends with me appreciating the scenery and thinking this wouldn't be a horrible way to die. I know it's morbid, but it's also beautiful, followed by a quick ending.

This jump was different, and not just because I had a bad exit. As I looked out across the Drop Zone (DZ), something hit me. It suddenly dawned on me that I was starting all over again. I had wanted to cry many times at the school but was never alone, so I kept it bottled up. Riding my canopy over the DZ was about as alone as it got. I let it all out. I started crying. No, not crying, bawling. Ugly-faced crying. I just kept saying to myself, "I do NOT want to be here. I don't want to do this shit anymore. I want to go home. I do NOT want to be here." I was done with starting over, keeping a positive attitude, being a good teammate to people who didn't know their shit but would pass anyway, people thinking I'm a tactical idiot because I couldn't pass a simple fucking patrol, teaching my peers and writing their orders for them while I failed time and time again, being told how impressive I was by the RIs and my fellow students just to be told I didn't know what I was doing when I got to the end of the field problem. I was done.

Then I landed like a sack of shit because I was lost in my own mind. I hit the ground with an audible thud. Feet, ass, elbows, and then head. And it was hard. I overpulled my slip (pulling down on the risers in a specific direction to help you land right), causing my body position to be 100 percent incorrect. I wiped my tears away and put my game face back on.

Prior to going to the DZ that day, I had harped on all the jumpers about what condition their equipment needed to be in upon reaching the end of the DZ. I even reminded a few people AGAIN as we walked off the field, "Have your rifle out with a magazine in as if you expect to come in contact as soon as you start moving!" That was the reality of what we were training to do. The 1SG told our company this was the first class in almost three years where everyone came off the DZ correctly. The guys seemed to think it was my doing.

NO ONE RESPECTS A SHEEP

On the bus to Darby, some dude sitting behind me decided he needed to get out before the rest of us once we got there. He hit me above my right eye with his gear, hard enough to bruise. I sprang up and roared expletives in his face. I could tell he didn't mean to by his reaction. My reaction was a lot, but sitting back and letting someone bruise your face without responding was not an option. We were a group of lions, not sheep. No one here respected a sheep.

As with many previous stages of my life, people asked me about being a woman in a predominantly male environment. My rehearsed snarky quip said that I had nothing to compare it to; therefore, I assumed it was the same as being a man. With regard to Ranger School, anyone who stuck out got more attention. And getting attention at a non-"gentlemen" school was never a good thing.

Even though I was bonding with this new group of guys, I was careful to maintain some distance. One thing I had learned quickly was if you are a woman among a bunch of dudes, keeping it slightly formal ensures certain barriers don't get crossed. So I still called everyone by their last names. If I don't know your first name, you can't possibly have illusions we will take our pass together. If you don't know my first name, your girlfriend won't make assumptions.

There were very few people I called by their first names who I knew from my military experience, even socially. If we were close, I gave them an endearing nickname. I'd take a bullet for you, but please don't use my first name. The depth and permanence of a military friendship cannot be replicated, yet there is this strange understanding of required distance, even when sharing a bunk bed. It's not explained but always understood. It's a perfect, inexplicable balance.

Thankfully, many of the RIs seemed to finally be over the fact that Kris, Shaye, and I were female students, which was a huge step in their professional development. Last time I went through Darby, I was the object of most of the RIs' anger, but not this time. I even smart-mouthed Hazemore when he reminded me this was my last chance, either pass or go home. Ol' SFC Hazemore saw me at an obstacle and made a beeline to me to make me do additional PT.

"Jaster, you better leave. I am sick of seeing you at Camp Darby."

I couldn't contain myself anymore, watching his uniform scream under the pressure of his huge midsection. I replied as loud as I could muster between gasps, "Roger that, Sergeant! Then fucking send me to MOUNTAINS!!!"

Hazemore fumed. Since my Ranger Buddy and I were the last on the course, all the RIs were gathering. The course NCO in charge let us skip a few obstacles just because I pissed off the one guy EVERYONE hated, RIs and students alike. It was once said, "If you want to test a man's character, give him some power and watch what he does with it" about Abraham Lincoln. This quote always comes to mind around Hazemore.

As long as gender mattered to someone, it was an issue. Now that RIs had stopped being weird about us being there, there may be a chance they would pass us. *Maybe we've passed all of their bro tests and finally proven ourselves.* It was possible that going through the entire first phase of the course twice, getting rated highly by our peers, taking a "Day One" restart when the male soldiers who were offered one declined, working our butts off for three weeks with minimal complaints, and then doing it all over again while getting better scores on almost every event was enough for people to understand we were both serious and competent.

What was scary about that was if I finally got graded on my merit and allowed to move on to Mountains, I would have to prove myself all over again with a new cadre. I couldn't handle three rounds in each phase. Even I am not that resilient.

GRADED PATROLS

I was the squad leader for a graded patrol on July 2. I was in charge of bay planning, and we had an officer for our RI. The OPORD went as smooth as butter. The coordination's briefing, where all four squad leaders come together to brief the cadre, ideally to deconflict missions, went okay—not great, not bad. Luckily, the other squads did horribly and embarrassed themselves during their briefings, so I looked better than I should have. Forty minutes after we started our mission, we had a lightning lockdown. We were near a random training building in the woods just outside the front gate, so we piled in for the storm and waited patiently, all snoring, until the "all clear" was called.

We moved a bit farther and then reacted to indirect fire. Someone lost his Ranger Handbook AND his helmet without realizing it. Luckily, I saw them and scooped them up. I tucked them in my ruck and kept moving without letting the RI know. The student could get in a lot of trouble for losing those.

We moved just a bit farther and then had another two-hour lightning lockdown. I napped as much as possible during each of the lockdowns. We completed an okay Linear Danger Area (LDA) crossing and then had an interesting react to contact. For some reason, I enjoyed this patrol. Maybe the stress was off, and I could just enjoy running around the woods. Home or Mountains: those were the only options. I was excited, and the mission felt good. I really do love soldiering.

On the twelfth day of Darby, July 3, I was carrying the Squad Automatic Weapon (SAW), which wasn't as heavy as the M240 but definitely added a few pounds and awkwardness. I don't want to EVER hear how I didn't pull my weight. This operation would be fun because I could unload on the enemy as they hit our ambush. Then we got an ammo resupply. Damn! We got a full combat load, again, plus everything left over from yesterday. The weight in my pack was crazy heavy, but overall, I felt good, and I was excited about this Darby. Third time's the charm, right?

Halfway through the day, I took over as the ATL for an ambush. The acting squad leader, Ski, was a super-intense guy. We butted heads quite a bit, but I still liked him. I placed the strong-side security position too close to our ambush, resulting in Ski saying I "fucked him." God, I hope not. After mission completion, our RI put us on the road immediately, and we conducted our AAR while walking because another lightning storm was coming. I took full ownership for poorly locating the security position and made sure the other students getting graded heard me. I felt terrible. We had flown through the recon and emplacement because prior to the recon, we had two lightning lockdowns. We wanted to get our link-up completed before the third lockdown. We made it to our spot, but another squad beat us to the designated location, so we ended up having to wait in the storm.

At my individual AAR, the RI said, "Don't worry, you'll get another chance at leadership." *Shit. I thought I did okay. ANOTHER failed patrol.* I know I messed up, but not nearly as much as 75 percent of the guys I saw blow through this course. Well, I guess I have a "No Go" for this one.

Every morning, I helped with the FRAGO. I was not the strongest Ranger—not the weakest either—but I was definitely a smart Ranger and the most experienced in this group. Hopefully, that would help me get through this school. I started thinking I might make it to Mountains—probably not beyond, but at least to Mountains.

But I was physically tired, my hip hurt, and I was carrying the M240 again. Fuck that twenty-seven-pound gun and running through the woods. There was another guy hurting almost as much as me, but he was only carrying an M4 and some squad equipment. I felt terrible. I ran out of water, felt dizzy, and wanted to puke.

I fell two to three times during the day movement. I was tired, carrying a shit ton, and not picking up my feet like I should. SF Jeff,[10] one of the group guys, pointed out some concertina wire, and I still managed to get my pant tie caught in it. I got both feet tangled up, tripped, and cut the back of my left calf. What a mess!!! SF Jeff said he loved following me. He knew exactly where not to step, day or night. "No question about footfalls when you are behind Jaster." Add that to my ego injury, and I let a little of the bitch come out a few times. I think I'm the only one who thought less of me for it, but I could not afford to show any weakness at all.

Despite my rollercoaster attitude and tired body, there were still fun days. One time, Ski and I were weak-side security for the ambush. The senior tactical leader from the schoolhouse accidentally drove his High Mobility Multipurpose Wheeled Vehicle (HMMWV), military vehicle, through our kill zone, so we killed his ass—and we did it with vigor! Thankfully, he was a champ and just played along. He jumped out of his vehicle and ran our way, so Ski and I mowed him down. I even screamed to simulate shooting a 320 round at him. Then the actual OP4 started walking toward the objective from our side—what was supposed to be our squad's

---

[10]   SF means Special Forces.

weak side. We laid into them too. It was SO worth carrying all the gear that day. I got to do something, and we had a ton of fun. My load was significantly lighter after all the rounds Ski and I shot. And the RI was impressed with our "violence of action." This was one of those days when playing soldier was a lot of fun.

The patrol base was more fun than usual as well. The squads were ridiculously close and not tactical at all. All of a sudden, we heard third squad firing off some M4 blanks, but there were no OP4. It is damn near impossible to negligent discharge (ND) (a.k.a. accidentally shoot your weapon) an M4.

Then, I heard someone yell that they saw a "rabid deer!" Yup, that's what they yelled, "Rabid Deer! Rabid Deer!" City folk. Then they yelled, "It's coming your way!!! Shoot!! Shoot!"

I finally yelled back, "We have blanks!"

LAST DAY AT DARBY

July 8 was the last day of my last Darby FTX. It was also my nine-teenth wedding anniversary. Somehow, I was the RTO, AGAIN!!!! Even the most sexist girl-hater couldn't talk shit about me now. I definitely carried my weight and then some. Literally! The calcula-tions didn't support randomization with regard to how much shit I was assigned by the cadre to carry—which was only exacerbated by my volunteering to carry shit to lighten the loads of my squad mates when they got fussy.

SF Jeff came over to visit with me as I set up my pack to carry the radio. I think he was half trying to cheer me up and half give me a dose of reality. He said, "Get ready for Mountains, Jaster. It's going to be heavier, harder, and longer hikes. You better be ready."

I smiled and hit him with a "Hoah!" but I refused to get my hopes up. I'd fallen off that cliff before.

The only good thing about being assigned the RTO on the last day was it was usually a good sign you had a "Go"! If I didn't, they would have given me another leadership position, and they never change RTO out midmission. Of course, what the fuck did I know about passing a phase?

Although I refused to get my hopes up about going to Mountains, there was still good news: after tonight's all-nighter writing Peers and cleaning gear, I would never again spend another night at Camp Darby. Of course, I had thought that before. Our RI for the day was a redheaded soldier who told me and Mouse (another Ranger student in our company) that he hated us both and wouldn't let us pass because he likes being the only "Ginger Ranger." That kind of familiarity was a subtle sign of acceptance.

As July eighth turned into July ninth, my RI called me up for my end-of-course counseling and looked like he had to pee. He hopped around as if the ground was on fire. His demeanor totally gave it away. I was a "Go"! Oh my GOD!!! Finally!!! Three Darbys and two RAP weeks, and I finally got a bus ride to Mountains. I found out all three female students got "Go"s.

An RI mentioned to me that a lot of people in the Ranger community were pissed we were moving on. But all our classmates and the RIs knew we deserved it. He reiterated that no one expected us to be able to handle the Mountains Phase. I wondered whether that share was to motivate or warn me.

The 1SG told us he was driving to Dahlonega, Georgia, with C-Co cadre to talk to his counterparts there personally. It was supposed to be his day off, but he wanted to make sure we didn't have to triple prove ourselves again and got a fair look. I guess taking that Day One recycle had won a lot of cadre over. The 1SG gave Shaye and I a nice little motivational speech. Then he called us ugly. Military signs of affection always made me laugh. Later on, when it was just the two of us, he said I had to succeed. His daughter was three years old. He wanted her to avoid all things Ranger—especially the men—but if she ever wanted to go to Ranger School, it was my job to make sure that could happen.

After brief elation from passing Darby Phase, I was now scared shitless. Everyone expected Mountains to "break us off." "Us" being the women. There were hundreds of posts about how no chick could last a day in a Mountains FTX. Time to test that theory.

CHAPTER 8

SHOW NO WEAKNESS

Mountains 1

July 11–July 31

It only took me twelve weeks to complete the first twenty days of Ranger School. My hips were tight, and both knees killed me. Fuck! I was so damn nervous. No, not nervous. Scared. If I were only three weeks from peak fitness instead of twelve, I may have had more confidence, but I had traipsed around the woods for almost three months. I didn't know if I had the strength left. What had I gotten myself into?

In Mountains, we would move as a platoon rather than a squad. Each infantry platoon consists of four squads, including two assault squads, a support by fire squad, and a weapons squad.

In Mountains, the graded leadership positions included platoon leader (PL), platoon sergeant (PSG), and four squad leaders (SL). The soldiers carrying radios, forward observer (FO) and radio telephone operator (RTO), and the two team leaders per squad (ATL and BTL) were critical roles but ungraded in this phase. The PL was overall in charge of everything that happened in the platoon. The PSG is second in command and is focused on administrative, logistics, and maintenance tasks. The SLs report to the PL and the TLs report to their respective SLs. The RTO usually follows the PSG but works for the PL, while the FO stays close to the PL. The PL and PSG would rotate three times per day while the four squad leaders would stay in position and be graded all day. The Mountains schedule was two days at lowers (training area at the bottom of a hill at Camp Merrill), climb Mount Yonah, two days at uppers (training on Mount Yonah), and five days at the planning bays doing PEs. Then we would wrap it up with a ten-day FTX. After that, we would out process and jump into Florida!

Our entire company in-brief went something like this: "We will fail or succeed as a platoon." Yup, that's it. *Holy shit. I better write that down! Greatest leadership school in the world!* I can't make this shit up.

THE CAMERA CREWS STRIKE AGAIN

We were up at 0400 on July 12. It was our first official day at Mountains Phase, and we were off to lowers. We ran all the way down the hill and then suffered through a lot of poorly taught classes on ropes and knots. But it wasn't all a waste; we completed three, thirty-foot repels off the tower and three rappels off of a sixty-foot wall. So much fun!

We finished up with some rappels off a ledge. I got several comments about my obvious air assault experience. The guys were all talking about how someday they would make a movie out of my Ranger School experience. Someone called me GI Jane. I laughed and used an Allan Jaster line, "Demi Moore pretended to be me." Of course, on my next trip down the side of the cliff, I had to yell, "GI Jane—on rappel!"

During one of my rappels, one of the SF guys was talking shit. I hollered back up while I was whizzing down, "Don't make me come back up there and kick your ass." I meant it in the most loving way.

The RI at the base of the cliff looked pissed at my lack of military bearing and wanted to know who the hell I was talking to. "That fussy Green Beret up there," I said and pointed.

Then he said, "I guess you fit in just fine, Ranger."

"Roger, Sergeant!!"

Unfortunately, *Combat Camera*, the organization within the Army that takes film and photos of soldiers in action all over the world, was all over Shaye and me. How much footage of stinky people with shaved heads did those damn TV cameras really need? We had a class on the one-rope bridge. Then we did a PE with two squads making the bridge while the rest watched (eight squads total). Afterward, we got smoked for some random reason. All the guys blamed the TV cameras; therefore, they blamed the women.

I agreed with the guys—I was pretty sure the RIs were showing off for the cameras.

At the base of Mount Yona.

On our third full day, we climbed Mount Yonah, which turned out to be a much smaller hike than I was expecting. We went into lightning lockdown several times, which meant the night rappel got canceled. That was disappointing, but it also meant more SLEEP!!! The rain, unfortunately, did not scare off CBS, NBC, *Combat Camera*, and the *Christian Science Monitor*.

I found out later that the *Christian Science Monitor* reported the redheaded woman ran to the front of the formation when the captain told weak ruckers to move forward. Allan updated me on the newspaper article, and it was awful. Absolutely awful. Allan was so pissed at me for not managing my image better. Of course, they hadn't asked for weak ruckers; they had asked for the short people to move forward. *Yup. Point taken. I gotta do better.* I fully understood the optics of showing any sign of weakness. Everything I did was being scrutinized. At this point, I just wanted to be a damn Ranger student and get this school over with. *Why can't people just let us be? I get it. I am a woman. Yup. I have been one for thirty-seven fucking years. I'm used to it. They should be too.*

FIELD EXERCISES

We conducted an ambush on our first of ten days in the field. It was supposed to be the hardest walk of the FTX, and I was the movement PL. I thought it was going to be a fairly easy position. We stayed on route thanks to an amazing point man. Our react to contact went well. It was tactically sound, but I could have used the M240 better, amassing more fire power. Then, we had a break in contact after a pretty decent LDA crossing, especially for the first day of the FTX. After the second squad crossed the road, they didn't half step or wait on the far side of the road. They just kept moving at a fast pace. I ran to the front because communications were down, and the hand and arm signals weren't working. When I got there, the point man had taken an unplanned turn due to vegetation. I stopped the front of the formation and went back and got the remaining part of the group. And just like that, I earned a "No Go" due to the break in formation. I failed my patrol because of something simple and almost completely out of my control.

I guess I had defeat and frustration written all over my face because everyone left me alone until I finally slept in the dirt at 0300.

The first day was all uphill, which meant the second day was mostly downhill. Easy movement, unless you have old knees and hips. After an 0530 breakfast MRE, we divided up gear. I carried the awkward but not heavy AT4 (a weapon that fires an 84 mm high-explosive anti-tank warhead through a tube). We conducted an ambush where we assaulted downhill, and we were reset because the mission went so horribly wrong. I thought the positioning was terrible, the instructions from student leadership were useless, and the follow-up during CASEVAC was a complete mess.

The RI asked me how I thought the mission should have been executed, even though I was not in a leadership position. I gave my answer, and he responded, "Damn, Ranger, you really do know your shit." He then stated he had heard a lot of good things about me. He told me to keep pushing, saying, "It's remarkable to see how much more you understand this stuff than most of the other students who come through here." He also highlighted how weird it was that I was so tactically sound but couldn't seem to get a "Go." Ya' don't say! My last three months summed up in two minutes.

I wasn't given one of the six maps our platoon had for this FTX because I was merely a member of the squad at this point. To keep mentally tuned in and stay in the moment, I kept a pace count and tried to track our azimuths. Daily, I wrote out the basic direction and distance in code on my hand to track movements. I earned a Minor Plus when an RI asked the platoon if anyone knew where we were. I asked to see the map he had taped around his walking stick and pointed to a spot based on terrain and how far I knew we had walked since the last major terrain feature. I got within two hundred meters and had the pleasure of shocking the hell out of the RI, who had assumed I was just droning through the movement. Two hundred meters isn't exactly a pinpoint, but it was pretty damn good for not having a map—or a lot of sleep. It was a huge ego boost for me and also a bit of a respect gainer for those around me who saw the events unfurl.

Day Three of our FTX was a "long walk" day. I knew what that meant. We planned to walk until the sun came up. I was the RTO again, and my pack was bursting at the seams with kit weighing close to one hundred pounds. The mission went well, and then we ate our evening MRE. I was excited until I realized that meant we had the famous "downed-pilot" mission as a follow-on before we could move to our patrol base. I was part of the rope team because I knew knots really well. Ski was also part of the rope team. Ski was a climber and indispensable in Mountains. Ski lead us through a damn-near-perfect execution, and I made sure everyone acknowledged the value he added.

After the downed-pilot mission, we kept a pretty solid pace until we hit our patrol base at 0345. Once we got to the site, the RI pulled gum wrappers out of his pocket he said soldiers from our platoon dropped along the route. The RI asked me how many squats we should do for each piece of trash he picked up. I said three because that was my daughter's age. He asked me how old my son was. Zac was six. We did six squats for every piece of trash.

I still had the radio on my back, and we did not drop our rucks before squatting. At one point, I literally just tipped over. I tried to stop myself, but it felt like I was living in a bad sitcom. We stood on a steep hill, so when I stood back up, I faced downhill. Of course, as the RTO, I was at the front and center of the formation with the leadership team, so there was no hiding in the shadows like most people were doing. They half-assed the exercise. I, of course, could not. My air squats with my ridiculous pack were parallel and more like back squats. And the next mission was uphill. We still weren't done for the night because we had to make sure we didn't lose any equipment on our walk. We didn't finish laying out our sensitive items until after 0400!

Thirteen days into Mountains, and we were on Day Four of our ten-day FTX. We got a whole twenty-five minutes of "sleep." We were released to eat and start rotating guard at 0405. It was 0430 when my watch went off—and I was the only one awake. That was awful. I was actually finishing my evening MRE when it was time to get up and start eating our morning MRE. I never closed my eyes that night. It was considered a safety violation to not eat your whole MRE, so I finished one and dove into the next. My stomach felt like I'd stuffed ten pounds of sand in a five-pound bag.

While I was in the prone on the perimeter, the RI shouted over to me to ask me how my legs were doing. I yelled back with a loud and boisterous, "You can't smoke a rock, Sergeant!" He then gave me a huge compliment about how well I did on the radio. The RI told me he and his support staff noticed I had the best communication they'd seen during an FTX. I'm going to take that as a win. It's hard to explain how it feels to get a compliment in Ranger School.

Day Five started with a bang. We were set up in a tactically terrible bowl-type area. It was exactly where you don't want a patrol base. Like, I actually think the Field Manual (FM) had a picture of this land formation with an "X" over it. Then the RIs brought in an OA. As soon as she rolled up, my squad mates groaned. They all figured getting a graded position with me guaranteed them a "No Go." The guys griped about how much harder the RIs were looking at fighting positions, checking on information distribution, and following checklists than they had the previous four days.

I was so sick of hearing, "Jaster, you know your shit, and you're a great team player, but being around you is a Ranger School kiss of death." The double standard was fucking killing me, both with grading and with building relationships. Guys on the outside kept bitching because the standards were getting lowered for women, but everyone on the inside knew the standards were more rigorous for the women. If the school would just stop fucking with the girls, we would fit in just fine and could be done with this damn experiment. Gender integration was only an issue for those on the outside looking in, and they ruined it for those of us actually in the arena. I wished they would get out of our way so we could just complete the damn mission!

As the day wore on, there was no doubt in my mind I was going to get a "No Go" for my planning PSG position. I screwed up a few really big things that had never been checked before (and I never saw checked again). The PSG weapon I was handed that morning had a spent round in the chamber, and like an idiot, I never checked it. The emergency evacuation locations were not properly disseminated after I gave them to the squad leaders. Someone left the wire without my knowledge. It was really difficult to motivate these guys when they were this tired and frustrated, especially since they assumed the days I got graded were automatic "No Go"s for everyone, no matter what they did. Their basic attitude was, "Why waste the effort when an OA is here?" I went around checking on all the fighting positions, and one guy told me to stop working so hard. "Jaster, you are the only person doing the right thing. That's going to exhaust you, and you still won't get your 'Go.'" *It's official. I have no more fucks to give. I am all out of fucks. I don't give a fuck!*

But I wasn't going to let a setback get me down. Another day, another chance at a "Go." On Day Seven of the ten-day FTX, we rolled back out to the field after receiving the OPORD briefing at 0800 and amazing hot chow. Blueberry pancakes! There were eleven guys in my squad total, and we were the weapons squad. We had three assigned to the platoon leadership as RTO, FO, and medic. That left us with only our squad leader and seven of us to carry both of the "big guns" and all their supporting equipment, such as tripods, extra barrels, and over two thousand 7.62 rounds. I was the M240 gunner, and we had an air INFIL, meaning helicopters would drop us off at our insert point. This was going to be a physically tough day since we were carrying three days' worth of food and a full combat load of ammo, and unfortunately, a map recon showed the contour lines around our insertion point were very close together! I dug extremely deep. I kept up, held my own, and even had fun ripping through some ammo during our mission. *Hoah! I get to be here! And that is badass!* I won't lie, my spirits got pretty low during the silent trudge of the march, with that big-ass gun and extra gear weighing me down physically and mentally, but I kept up and was proud of myself for being there and continuing down a path many had failed before me.

Day Eight of our FTX, and I was struggling. I had definitely overextended myself the day before, and we had a huge climb during our movement. I fell to the back of my squad. I was doing fine, and most of the guys had a rough day after they carried the big gun too. But a rough day plus the big hike plus people looking for a reason to look down on me made for a wicked combo.

Another officer in the platoon, Dash, lead the squad that was in the rear. For some reason, he decided he wanted to walk the two rear squads abreast of each other—I have no idea why. This wasn't a normal movement pattern, nor was it directed by the PL or PSG. Dash's squad starting walking next to our squad instead of behind it. As soon as his squad did not follow the path the first three squads had walked, it looked as though I had fallen to the rear of the formation. I hadn't; the rear took a different route. But it was all about optics.

The RI threatened me with an SOR when we got to the top. My closest friend in the squad could tell something was wrong the minute he saw me at my fighting position. I told him what happened, and he flew over to Dash and threatened to kick his ass. Dash felt terrible once he realized what he had done. Even he couldn't figure out why he chose to take a different path during the movement—mark it up to exhaustion. He came over to chat, and I was not in a forgiving mood. Bad on me. Dash was one of the good ones, the really good ones. He often didn't understand why people struggled at the things he found easy, but he listened, worked hard, and genuinely wanted everyone to succeed. That minirift stuck with us for a couple days. It was my issue. If I hadn't appeared weak, I would have never ended up in that position in the first place. Pride was VERY hard to swallow.

On Day Nine of the Mountains FTX, I was the assault one squad leader. A third time being in a graded position solidified what I already suspected: I didn't have a "Go." That sucked. We traveled over six more kilometers after our movement to contact, mission completion, and clear the objective. That might not seem like much, but the mountains of Dahlonega, Georgia, were not forgiving. I ran my ass back and forth throughout my squad formation and my SF medic buddy's squad because they kept falling back. He was not pushing his squad hard, but I didn't want to risk losing anyone since a break in contact was the one thing that had cost me more "Go"s than anything else at Ranger School. I actually ended up heading all the way to the front of the formation as well because everyone was droning and losing consciousness while they were walking. It really was crazy to see that many people sleeping on their feet and still moving.

After that performance, I was certain I had gotten a "Go." I didn't know how I couldn't. I was all over it, controlled the formation, knew what was going on, and made sure to keep everyone together. If the RIs looked at the whole leader, even if I screwed a few small things up, there was no way I wouldn't move on to Florida. Also, when I wasn't in a graded position, I was the "go-to" Ranger for a lot of things. I was called into the center to help write the order daily. I carried gear almost every day or volunteered for a leadership position. The RIs complimented my tactics. I couldn't imagine not being "good to go."

We slept on a crazy-steep hill that night, and I was sliding just sitting down. I set my ruck at my feet to keep from slipping down the hill. Some of the guys actually tied themselves to trees. It was getting a bit chilly at night, so I pulled out the thin layer of my sleeping bag, undressed, and got in. Once in my bag, I got stung by something. Then I got stung again. Apparently, I had lain on a hive for ground bees. I was too exhausted to relocate, so I just pulled my sleeping bag all the way over my head and went to sleep. Throughout the night, I got a couple more stings, including two on my face, but I didn't care.

It was the last day of the FTX!!!! I didn't have an assigned job, and, minor miracle, no one loaded me up with gear. So I volunteered to be the BTL. For our final mission in Mountains, my team was on security. My RI gave me a quick, bullshit review and then told me to go away because he couldn't look at my face. *I guess at thirty-seven, I just don't have it like I used to!* I didn't realize until later, when I was applying cammo, that the bee stings on my face had swelled up significantly, and I looked like a complete freak show!

ANOTHER
DISAPPOINTMENT

When we got back to Camp Merrill, 1SG pulled me aside and said, "I respect the hell out of you for coming." That was a huge compliment because I didn't get the impression he was on the "let the girls try" bandwagon in the beginning. This was definitely a "hearts and minds" campaign when it came to cadre.

All the guys wanted to know what the 1SG said to me. When I told them, they all started cheering, thinking I was definitely a "Go" to Swamps. I tried not to get my hopes up, but let's be honest, if I didn't pass this phase and others did, there was absolutely no "standard."

Each Ranger student was individually called in for their counseling with the company cadre. The RI told me my Peers were lower than usual but not bad. He then stated I needed to make sure they didn't fall during the next phase, or I could be at risk of not graduating. Finally, he mentioned something about what I needed to improve for Florida, stopped himself, and paused for a long, contemplative moment. I was immediately disappointed my Peers dropped while simultaneously elated I was moving on. My mind instantly focused on Florida.

The RI's face contorted. Then he regained his composure and commented, "First, you will get another try in Mountains." Wait. What? It was almost as if he knew I was "Go" and seeing the word "recycle" on my sheet surprised the shit out of him.

My heart sank. I was shocked. My patrols weren't perfect, but that last one was pretty damn close. I couldn't even imagine what went wrong. I was completely and utterly dumbfounded.

Kris and Shaye both moved on. The rumors of fairness started immediately. I was furious. *You want to talk about fair? Tell me how I could get RIs in my first Darby and my first Mountains Phase attempts telling me I should be moving on, and then I get recycled anyway? How the hell was that fair? If you were looking for "fair," go somewhere else. Suck it up, shut up, and leave me alone.*

CHAPTER 9

THEME

Mountains 2

August 1–August 28

During my time as a recycle between my first and second attempts at Mountains, after one of my many chow-hall details, an OA stopped me. These discussions never went well, so I braced for impact and waited for whatever weird interaction we were about to have.

She surprised me when she said, "Jaster, I know it's hard to be left behind. The story of two fit, young warriors successfully completing leadership training is fine, but it's nothing compared to your story. Don't ever hang your head. Women like me want to see you succeed more than you know and more than we can tell you. You go, mamma. Now get the fuck out of my face."

More emotions I couldn't deal with right then, so the roller-coaster continued.

Time to press reset—again.

INTEGRATION WOES CONTINUE

One day, after PT, I had to head to the medical clinic (TMC) because the colonel, a senior officer not located at Camp Merrill, heard I was injured. I was so annoyed because there was no reason an O-6 should care about a Ranger student's sick call. Please show me the person who's been through this course and never limped. If I needed a sick call, I could walk my happy ass there myself. Oh yeah, and none of the limping men were forced to go to TMC!

After my appointment, I checked in with the RI on duty. He asked me what was wrong that I had to go see the doc. I told him my gender seemed to be the problem. In a random venting session, I let my guard down long enough to tell him the forced doctor visits were almost as divisive as their barracks integration-through-segregation policy. I went off on a tirade about how the only people who make women at Ranger School an issue are those that aren't actually involved in Ranger School. None of the students cared that I was a female student. After working with me, none of the RIs seemed to care either. But people in DC or reading the newspaper REALLY cared—about stupid stuff—and were making my life worse whenever possible.

The Training Command (TRADOC) policy stated I needed

to sleep separate from the guys while not in active training. Well, the Ranger School barracks on the tiny post at Camp Merrill were NOT set up for that. They only had huge, open bays. I was placed, by myself, on the second floor. I explained this was the most dangerous course of action for me because when I slept in the same room as the guys, it was a safe environment full of my classmates and peers who had looked out for me and each other for the past six weeks. The school made me easy prey by leaving me isolated and without a way to defend myself. The previous night, some drill sergeants using the other side of the barracks had been drinking and talking and just being soldiers. I had no idea if they were good people, and I couldn't afford to find out. One too many beers, too much time away from a spouse, or someone who was strongly opinionated about women in Ranger School could ruin my life, not just my attempt to earn the tab. The RIs never thought about it that way. Thankfully, they listened patiently and were hit with the stark reality of what my day really looked like. I just wanted to be a student and pass this damn course. If higher-ups stopped trying to make things "safe" for me, I could fit in with the guys and actually be safe. Policymakers singled me out and put me at risk because they were fucking clueless.

When no one was watching over the students, although my adjectives allowed me to take a unique approach to various situations, the guys seemed to find it completely normal for me to pipe in about extremely uncomfortable topics. While we were all waiting in line to call home before the guys moving on to Florida left, I overheard a young man talking about potentially having to medically recycle, as his "member" had rubbed raw, and he wasn't sure how he would be able to take the constant movement through water for the Swamps ten-day FTX. I am certain he was mortified when I turned around and offered a creative solution involving the soft case from our issued safety glasses as a hammock attached to the buttons of his fly by the case's draw string. A few weeks later, he was the class honor graduate and thanked me in a video for my "motherly" advice that, in his words, "Allowed me to fight on to the Ranger objective."

But I have to admit that every once in a while, being a woman was the source of some fun too. For example, one time Allan sent me an extremely creative care package. Ranger students were authorized almost anything except porn, cigarettes, caffeine, and alcohol. The prohibited list included specific magazine titles that regularly featured naked or mostly naked women. But nothing was mentioned about sending mostly naked men. Therefore, Allan plastered the inside of my box with pictures of male strippers in camouflage, firefighting gear, and similar barely-there costumes. He had stuck on little call outs from all the guys saying things like, "Hey, Jaster, how about I join you on some night ops?" and, "I'll be your Ranger Buddy!" The RIs inspected every box before they gave them to the students. After they opened mine, I could tell immediately there was an issue. A crowd of RIs gathered, and heads began to shake. They looked at the contents of the box, then at me, then back at the box. Finally, the senior RI blushed and handed it over to the staff sergeant on duty. He laughed until his cheeks were red and threw it out the door of the mail room saying, "Jaster, come get this bullshit." They couldn't decide if they should punish me or put me on a pedestal. Either way, my box was the topic of conversation for the rest of the day.

Care package my husband made for my Mountain's Recycle.

CRUSHING IT IN CLASS

While sitting through yet another class I'd already taken, my blood started to boil, and I couldn't seem to calm down. I realized I had failed, but academically, I was good. I knew this stuff by heart—like backward, forward, and every which way. When we completed PEs, I got little to no critiques from the RIs and accolades from my fellow recycles. I didn't know how much more of this bullshit I could take.

While I was at Camp Merrill, Zac, my baby boy, turned seven. I was stuck at Ranger School, never moving forward—just on a treadmill of misery while my babies grew up. *Fuck this place.* I knew I needed to finish strong, but these events messed with my soul. *I just need to stay focused. I am Ranger Jaster, not Mom or Lisa.*

Once I got my head in the game, I did well. I learned more this time around. I was able to help my classmates. And we ended on simple and complex rope systems. It was good training and a little fun. I was pleasantly surprised at how much I remembered from the last cycle.

When we hiked up Mount Yonah, the A-Co commander led the way. We lined up by height, so I was second in line. I'm not sure if it was because we were in a different company or because it wasn't quite as hot, but from the base of the mountain to the landing zone (LZ), we went notably faster and carried significantly more weight than last time. I made sure to stay in perfect step with the guy in front of me. To keep a formation moving at a consistent pace, maintaining proper distancing at all times, regardless of terrain, is paramount.

But as we headed up the steepest part of the mountain, I didn't feel like I could keep the current pace. I counted as I let fourteen people pass me. I didn't want to be the cause of any gaps because not making the timed cutoff meant having to redo the march the next day and a Major Minus. I was not about to be a Blue Falcon (a.k.a. Buddy Fucker). As we walked the final stretch, the RI near the front of the formation started counting down the seconds from about fifteen. Oh shit! We were all shocked, and everyone within earshot sprinted the last bit of the mountain. It was obvious no one knew about the cutoff, as only twenty-five of us finished in the required allotment of time, and twenty-nine, more than half, didn't. This was an easy walk for most of the failures, but since they didn't know TODAY's "Ranger Standard," they would walk to the base at 0400 the very next day and redo the entire thing. Everyone was pissed. Not only did we not know the standard, we also weren't allowed to wear watches, so we couldn't have paced ourselves even if we had known. The other companies each only had a handful of failures, just like last cycle. It sounded like we had an instructor problem, not a student problem.

The very next training event forced us to walk almost to the bottom of the mountain and build complex rope–pulley systems to drag mock bodies up the incline. Our PEs brought us almost halfway up the mountain, but after our lunch MRE, we had to ruck the rest of the way to the top—the hardest portion of the climb. We got to camp at 1600, cleaned weapons, and changed our socks. We had another MRE around 1745 and chapel service at 1900. I needed that. I realized finishing this out the right way meant I got to be with my family and hold my head up, but I had to remind myself of that a lot more now than I did before. Five more weeks. Only five short weeks until I drove back from Florida to Camp Rogers to graduate. *God, give me the strength to make it to the finish line.*

After chapel, training continued with a two-hundred-foot night rappel. We got back to the parking lot after 0100. Then we retied ropes, got sensitive items inspected, and finally slept. The Yonah-climb redos had to be up at 0330. To maximize their sleep, they literally ran down the mountain. On the second attempt, six failed. This was a mandatory pass event, but since it was such a high percentage, they only got Major Minuses. Yup, that elusive "Ranger Standard."

DON'T LET THE QUIT IN

My alarm went off at 0505 on August 14. The bay was dead. Surprise, as usual, guard had failed, and I apparently had the only functioning watch alarm. I started barking immediately! Someone literally turned on the lights seconds before the RI walked in, and everyone faked it well enough that it looked like we hadn't overslept. That was a close one. Had the RIs caught us oversleeping, it would have been a much more painful day!

When Class 9-15 arrived, their class leader was a dude I knew from Vaughn's Platoon during the three-week summer recycle session. He had been our class leader as Kris, Shaye, and I prepared to insert as Day Ones. He was a good guy and seemed extremely squared away. He had failed Darby a second time after I moved on. I assumed he had been sent home; therefore, seeing him not only get off the bus, but then also as the class leader shocked me. This school was rough, but leadership sleeps less, eats last, and gets shit from everyone, students and cadre. I finally had a chance to chat with him. He said he double "No Go"ed patrols and was a drop. When he went in for his Brigade Board, he asked Colonel Fivecoat for a Day One restart because, according to him, he was inspired by the Athena 3. That lifted my spirits. Being here sucked, but his comments made me remember why I stayed: to change hearts and minds. Motivation returned thanks to an old friend.

I volunteered for PSG on August 16 during our PEs. Students had two attitudes toward recycles. They either believed recycles had been there before and you could learn from them, or they believed nothing a recycle said should be trusted because they were failures. The assigned PL thought the latter and impressed no one with his assumptions. His attitude changed very quickly when even the asshole RI repeatedly told me I was right and he was wrong in front of the platoon. He finally started listening when the entire platoon wanted to know why he was so jacked up and not a team player. That subtle torque of changing one person's attitude ultimately changed the dynamic of the entire platoon.

At breakfast that day, I heard that one woman passed Florida. Whoever it was, they will be a military name to remember. *The first woman to graduate Ranger School. Epic. I wish it had been me, not just because I wanted to be the first, but because it would mean*

I was done! Both Kris and Shaye were exactly the type of soldiers who should be in history books.

Leadership was rolled out around 1500. I did not get a position. I was pissed. Bay planning was officer shit and the stuff I needed to be graded on since it was what I actually did. Instead, the chaplain was the PL. A man of God was far from the best choice to plan tactical movements and operations. I was certain he was going to pass, and that made this one of those times when it was hard not to be frustrated with Ranger School and its imaginary "standards." Ranger Regiment and other high-speed units needed chaplains who were Ranger qualified. I get it. It's still frustrating, but I get it.

I survived the first day of the FTX. Conner Mountain followed by Sassafras Mountain had me praying for a rolled ankle or snake bite because dropping from a rattlesnake or copperhead bite would be dignified. I dragged my feet a bit, hoping a snake or even a rock would attack me, but no such luck. So I put my head down, kept moving, and resolved that quitting was STILL not an option. My brain flashed to an episode of *The Ultimate Fighter* from 2013 when Ronda Rousey sat outside a steam shower telling her athlete to never let the quit in. I decided to adopt that as my motto: "Don't let the quit in." Because, as Rousey explained it, once quit gets a foot in the door, it's always there.

BEING A TEAM PLAYER

After settling into my position, I spotted a vehicle on the road. We unleashed hell immediately. The poor 5th RTB chaplain was just coming by to check on troop morale. He did his job well because my morale definitely improved! My heavy trigger finger lightened my ruck load by a few pounds, and I got to blow off some frustration by shooting what I thought was an "enemy." Then another vehicle drove up. I assumed this was the actual enemy, but the RIs played it off well, and we acted as though the second vehicle was the chaplain's reinforcements. So we blew the claymore and shot the AT4. It was so much fun! I assumed the chaplain was most likely right with God. I felt no remorse sending him on his way.

Rain all day combined with another pending storm meant the RIs shortened our hike. The RIs, carrying much less gear, rushed us over extremely awful terrain. I slid HARD on the wet underbrush and wasn't sure I was going to be able to get back up. I knocked my breath out with that one. To add insult to injury, once we all started slipping, we had to wear our helmets to avoid potential head injuries; normally, we patrol in our soft caps until we execute the assigned mission. At one point, during the movement to our camp, we stopped and put a classmate, Forrest, on the SkedCo. He let himself get dehydrated, so we carried him down the hill to a road for FLA pickup, and then we hiked back up the mountain. I volunteered to be on the team that took him down to the truck. I was originally worried about him, but some of his squad mates from Darby informed me Forrest got similarly "dehydrated" during the last phase, and they didn't believe he was doing much more than taking some time off from training. If that was true, he could expect a reckoning to follow.

Later, Forrest returned to the patrol base before we stepped off, so we were back to full strength. The ground was still slippery, and everyone stepped gingerly during our first movement of the day. One student fell completely backward as we climbed the mountain, turning just enough to land straight on his head, hard. He had to be evacuated via helicopter due to fear of a spinal injury. As acting PSG, I took charge of the helo evac. I expected the RI to take over communication, but he let me run the entire evac. When the helo lifted off, the RIs gave us a minute to readjust. The platoon was still concerned about the dude who fell when Forrest, our "dehydrated" classmate, started acting loopy, speaking non-sense and having problems forming sentences. Each Mountain Phase, the students have to conduct a down-pilot mission. Forrest became our downed pilot, and we used him instead of the dummy. I think the dummy had better people skills. We moved him two kilometers, including conducting a river crossing and climbing a large hill/small mountain. Everyone in the platoon wanted to drop Forrest in the river or off the cliff. During the movement and all the commotion, I swapped out of my leadership position. But even after getting replaced, I felt responsible for the platoon. I wanted to stay involved because a lot had happened, and if the new person was droning earlier in the day, people could really get lost or hurt. For me, teamwork didn't end with a patrol; it was always. That's how the real Army works, and that's the soldier I wanted to always be.

The RI pitied us and moved our objective closer. Then he walked us directly, and slowly, to our patrol base. It started raining again and never stopped. I shared a hooch with two guys. We couldn't hear or see anything, so my hooch mates and I conducted a foot cleaning and family dinner under our expedient "field house." We giggled like teenagers at an *Adams Family* pedicure parlor. We actually heated up our meals and traded sides. I think we even sampled each other's "recipes." And then, we got six hours of sleep! During my AAR, I asked the RI why he was being so lenient. He said that after two real-world casualties in one day plus three days with minimal sleep, bad rain, and cold weather, we were headed for more injuries if our company didn't get some rest. The RIs were actually worried about us.

Based on my conversations with the RIs and how I not only took care of my Ranger School business but also the actual casualties, I was pretty confident I got a "Go." Again, if I could handle all this real-world shit while playing pretend army, I had what it took to bear the tab. Of course, I had that thought previously and was dead wrong.

I was the FO carrying one of two large radios for Day Four of our ten-day FTX. We conducted a raid that required us to call in a helo for High Value Target (HVT) first aid and extraction. It was a high-speed mission. Unfortunately, the poor specialist who was the RTO was a young medic in the active Army without much radio experience. He could not get the commands right for calling the bird into our location. I quickly wrote out EXACTLY what he needed to say and snuck the paper to him. He looked at me with pleading eyes and handed me the mic. He said, "You have better eyes on the LZ." We both knew what that meant. I made the call.

I wanted to help my buddy and make sure he didn't get in trouble for not knowing how to do his job, but luckily, rather than giving him a Major Minus, the RI gave me a Major Plus.

At mission completion, the RI let us sit on our rucks and eat an MRE. That was ALWAYS a bad sign. It felt like they were saying, "Your mission went so badly, we are just going to go admin for a bit to unfuck you guys." If we didn't tank the mission, it meant we were about to walk until sunlight or hit a second objective. This time, we were headed back to base camp to refit.

I volunteered to be a team leader on our next mission. At the end, the squad leader thanked me and said he knew I would work myself to death rather than let him get a "No Go." The next day, the RI told me I got another Major Plus for my efforts as a team leader. Hell, yeah!

On the sixth day, I was the weapons squad leader. I really thought it went well. The mission went amazing, and then there was a follow-on mission resulting in a helo medivac. Basically, I responded to two totally different combat missions during my graded period rather than the usual one. The RI was shocked after asking me to pinpoint our location in the middle of a movement when I stopped, grabbed my map, grabbed a blade of grass, and was spot on—with no pauses or contemplation. The RI complimented me on knowing where we were at all times, doing an extremely thorough recon, and conducting expert weapons emplacement. He was a weapons squad leader before coming to the schoolhouse, and he had nothing but praise for everything I did. He admitted to grading me really hard.

But then, during the AAR, the RI said there was a casualty from fratricide no one mentioned the night before. How can no one die during the mission and then after the end of the exercise, we get told there was a casualty? That meant I was a "No Go" for sure. It was easier for the RI to make some shit-ass excuse to fail me than give me the "Go" I deserved for the tactical competence HE said HE witnessed.

The next day, our young medic who I helped call in the helo was the squad leader. We all wanted to get him a "Go." He had so little experience but the heart of a lion. Unfortunately, based on how they graded me yesterday, I assumed he didn't have a snowball's chance in hell of passing. He didn't recon the positions for either M240. He didn't personally emplace his guns or check their sighting once they were set. He didn't give his gunner left and right limits or a Final Protective Line (FPL). He also neglected to put in rear security. Of course, the RI told him right then and there, at the end of his mission, that he got a "Go." I thought, *I'm happy for my Ranger buddy, but FUCK this place.*

ANOTHER TWIST IN THE RIDE

We were on the final days of our FTX, and I was done. The emotional rollercoaster was real, but I had headed steadily down for way too many days in a row to come out of this swan dive. I had to get my mind right. I was either headed to Swamps in a few days or headed home. Either way, my fate was sealed, and I was leaving Camp Merrill. Damn, that statement sounded familiar.

I got assigned as planning PL. Finally! This should be too easy, except someone claimed they didn't get the right number of MREs after our food resupply the night before. The security the previous leadership set up was shoddy at best. So I had two major tasks on top of my planning duties that no one else had to worry about when they were graded as PL. We were also INFILing today by helo, and the student PSG did not put together the flight manifest (list of people and equipment flying). He literally got nothing accomplished all morning. Since he didn't do his job, I had to do both. And if I did them both well, I knew he would get a "Go"— and most likely, I would get another "No Go" because...Ranger School. I had little time to prep and brief my FRAGO, making up my plan seconds before the words came out of my mouth. I hoped it sounded convincing.

Coming off a PL position the first part of the day, I returned to my squad after the leadership changeover. The student assigned as squad leader on our last day in the field was a complete shit bag —he was all gung-ho while in leadership and lazy as hell when he wasn't. He hadn't volunteered to do a damn thing, and no one wanted to help him get his "Go." But hey, I was not them, so I did what my peers wouldn't: step up and take charge as a team leader. We stepped off, and the RI fired me as soon as we started moving because he realized I was in a leadership position again. He said, "Someone else needs to do something in this damn platoon." I started hoping that was foreshadowing but couldn't let myself feel good just to endure another big crash.

As we were coming down the mountain, the RI let it slip that

I WAS A "GO"!!!!!! OMG!!!!! This was epic. Based on his comments, this was a highly supported decision, and many of the RIs were happy to see me move forward with Class 9-15. The RI indicated that given the opportunity, he and his peers would gladly serve with me in the field. They believed I truly embodied the Ranger Creed. My heart swelled—as did my eyes, just a little. There are no sweeter words in the military than, "I'd share a foxhole with you."

My last night at Camp Merrill, an RI pulled me aside. He said a lot of people were rooting against me, but there were quite a few behind me. He said I got my "Go" all on my own, but the team really did want to set me up for success. I'm guessing the unwritten message was I got graded hard to ensure no one could question the validity of my success should I make it to Victory Pond.

Right after our final outbrief, the Battalion Commander pulled me aside. "Do not draw attention to yourself." Well, shit. Thank you for those powerful words of wisdom. I stuck out like a sore thumb: old, female, and the only one with hair on my head—red hair at that!

CHAPTER 10

THREE, TWO, ONE, GO!

Swamps 1

August 29–September 13

I was finally headed to Swamps! I was ready to pass at least one phase as a first-time "Go."

I was focused and ready. I chanted to myself, "Three, two, one, go," which stood for three trips through Darby, two through Mountains, one through Florida, and then I want to get the hell out of this place.

SAME SHIT, DIFFERENT DAY

On August 29, we were up by 0230 and on the bus by 0330. We stayed at the hangar for an hour before they finally canceled our jump into Swamps due to high winds—so we drove to Florida. Fully drooling, snoring, and mouth breathing along with all my brothers in suffering, we arrived at Camp Rudder at 1330. The bus ride had been a nice respite from the chaos, but that changed quickly. As soon as we hit the ground, we were loading ammo.

There were sixty-plus recycles in our company. That was a HUGE recycle rate for Swamps and almost quadruple the average, according to school historical stats.[11] I guess the curse of the women Rangers was alive and well. The added attention we brought RAISED, not lowered, the standards, yielding more recycles and a lot of bitter men. My squad received three recycles.

Since it was the third and final stage of Ranger School, we jumped right into training. During our first PE, I was assigned as the RTO (carrying the radio again) for the first two movements. Then I traded off and carried the rope. It seemed I was continually assigned extra equipment by the RIs. I guess that was good because even when I wasn't getting tasked with the big stuff, I made sure to volunteer to carry more than my fair share so no one questioned my ability, strength, or resolve. And when I wasn't carrying more, I volunteered for additional duties. For example, when we practiced boat operations and rope bridges, I got to be the strong swimmer: the lead soldier who swims the rope across a river and then ties it to a tree on the far side so others can cross attached to the rope. The shocked looks on the RIs faces when my squad chose

---

11   Jason, "About Ranger School," By the Numbers (blog), Blogger, accessed October 7, 2022, http://bythenumbersblog.blogspot.com/p/about-ranger-school.html.

the "girl" were priceless. They too would come to understand I was an excellent swimmer, good at organizing my team, and willing to volunteer for critical additional assignments.

On the day we were to start our FTX, the new chain of command for our first mission was called out at 0630. Unfortunately, my name was not called for the first round of leadership assignments. I wanted a position up front because ten days with no break made the last couple days difficult. I had had three patrols in Mountains with only one "Go." Thankfully, I had gotten multiple "Go"s in Darby. I needed to succeed early and often to maintain the 50 percent "Go" rate required to graduate.

I became the PL in the afternoon of the second day. I was told the patrol base was okay and we had a good movement. Noise and light discipline were poor at times, but overall, individual soldier discipline was good, and my violence of action was a plus. There were some areas where we could improve, such as platoon communication, but that wasn't necessarily on me.

However, I was told we had committed fratricide, which was an automatic "No Go." I couldn't understand how no one in the entire platoon knew we had a fratricide. How could this possibly happen on another one of my patrols? No one else had these mysterious, unknown fratricides, while I seemed to have multiple while working with the exact same people, moving in the exact same formations. The squad leaders who apparently shot each other both got "Go"s, and the PSG also thought he passed. So let's run back through that: The RI said there was a fratricide event. The student in charge of the group of soldiers that did the shooting got a "Go."

The student in charge of the group that got shot got a "Go." My second in command, the student in charge of the formation, got a "Go." But I got a "No Go." You can't be vengeful and successful at the same time—but damn I fought to keep my head on straight.

It was only Day Two, but as the army cadence goes, "Here we go again. Same ole shit again."

HOPE

We were taking UH-60s helos to the insertion point and we got chow birds! "Chow birds" were when the pilots pitied the Ranger School students and snuck us food during our mission. The RIs knew it happened but looked the other way. Not every helicopter crew did it. Money for the food had to come out of their own pockets. Luckily, our crew believed in the tradition. Our helo had two Little Caesars pizzas for only seven of us!!! We ate until we wanted to puke. The fact that those pilots would do that made me love the Army so much. Think about it. These guys and gals were complete strangers who spent their own money to give a little bit of joy to those of us slugging it out in Ranger School. Pure, unadulterated generosity for no other reason than "helping out a buddy." What an amazing tribe I belong to!

One guy's mom died while we were in the field. I know I wouldn't have handled it as well as he did. He left the field for a day and a half and then was right back in the fight. I didn't really know him, but he was just a baby, and the outcome of this school would decide his fate in the military. He needed this, but he also needed to be with his kid sister during this horrible time. His mom had been sick off and on for a while but had been doing okay when he left for Ranger School. Her death was a real shock for him.

I sat with him and simply said, "I don't know you, and I know nothing about your troubles. But I am here for you and am more than willing to be a sounding board if you ever want to just tell someone stories who wants to listen." He teared up but then fought through it. He told me that was the nicest thing anyone had said to him.

One night, while we were prepping for a mission, he told me that while he was in the battalion headquarters at Camp Rudder, he heard the RIs talking about me. He swore I had a "Go" and said everyone was really impressed with my physicality after such a long stay at Ranger School. He said some of the RIs commented that the male students should be embarrassed that some support woman knew more about tactics than they did. Hopes were high again.

I was also getting signs that the RIs were accepting me as just another member of the team. One day, when the OP4 probed the patrol base, I saw them first. I popped up and "shot" the M320 (grenade launcher). The RI said that was "hot." He immediately blushed, remembering where he was, who he was, and who I was. After an awkward silence, we all giggled. His reaction was awesome and genuine. I loved it. Stuff that outsiders thought was weird or inappropriate worked for us. Imagine if one of those reporters had overheard the comment and reported it. The Army would have been publicly castrated, and the RI who said it would have been kicked out for sexual harassment. But without the media and "socially approved" vernacular, we were just a bunch of "dudes" executing a kick-ass mission and getting excited by the outcome. I took it for what it was: a compliment.

For one of my graded missions, we had a five-kilometer boat movement followed by six hundred meters in the swamp. I got switched into the PSG role after the worst guy on the squad had been our squad leader. Fuck my life. He hadn't disseminated anything. Literally, I had ZERO idea of the mission, objective, movement—nada. I had to learn everything on the spot but pulled a successful mission out of my butt. The RI threw in a lot of complicated scenarios. The other students were stunned at the complexity of my mission compared to theirs. I figured it was because we were so late in the FTX, but apparently, he was testing me.

My counseling after that graded patrol went okay. We "chatted" a lot. The RI said he tried hard to make the AAR sound like neither a "Go" nor a "No Go." He asked me a lot about my personal motivation. I wasn't sure where he fell on the integration continuum. I got the impression that even though he was my grader, he himself didn't know if I was a "Go" or not.

On September 10, I was assigned as a team leader again. I was not sure if that was a good or bad sign. I felt like I might have a "Go" since I did not get another graded position; I'd heard that gossip from my buddy whose mom died; and my team really trusted me to take charge tactically. I started letting myself get excited about graduation and seeing my family. The end felt near. Three-two-one-GO!

IF I DIDN'T HAVE BAD LUCK

Our second Swamps movement was called "The Weaver." Since we were security squad, we led the way. The young medic from Hawaii was the squad leader. He begged me to take point: "Jaster, you always spot the OP4 early, and you're good at land nav." So I did.

We got stuck behind another platoon during our boat movement and had a two-hour lightning lockdown, so we ended up hitting the rope-bridge site after dark. As usual, I was the "strong swimmer" as well as point man. After swimming the rope across the river and getting everyone to the other side pretty damn quickly, even in the dark, we walked through the swamps. I sunk in the muck up to my hips a couple times. Being a "pocket Ranger" definitely had its downsides. I kept us on track pretty well. The RI kept trying to get me to rush the platoon's pace while I was at point because events earlier in the evening had busted our timeline, but I refused to let people get separated in the swamps this late at night for an arbitrary hit time. Although the RI was getting anxious, he understood and appeared to appreciate the fact that I was thinking about the big picture and still communicating well. I maintained a rather good attitude and mental acuteness through my fifth month at a two-month school, and people, including cadre, seemed to notice.

The next day, the RI called my name for leadership. My heart sank, as I was worn out after running point while navigating through the swamp the evening before. Being point meant my performance had had a HUGE impact on whether or not my buddy had gotten his "Go," so it felt like I had leadership two days in a row. Luckily, we were weapons squad, and I knew my shit with regard to that position. Unfortunately, the Ranger students picked to be my PL and PSG were both unimpressive at best. It would be a challenge, but those positions changed out before mission execution, so there was a chance.

As my mother says, if I didn't have bad luck, I would have no luck at all. Just before we started the mission, I got switched from weapons squad leader to assault squad leader. I adjusted and remained flexible. Changing my job at the last minute happened a few too many times to me and never to anyone else to be coincidental. When the new RIs came in, the PL and PSG never put out a black-and-gold plan (withdrawal routes should we get overrun). The entire patrol base looked terrible and was basically a "No Go" for all the leadership. I would have to do everything else perfectly to pass, and we were scheduled to do the Santa Rosa mission, a.k.a. "No Go" Island. Santa Rosa is either a boat or helo movement to a prestaged mock city on an island. It was known to be a fun mission, but also one that always got screwed up.

However, one of the helos broke down, and we couldn't get to Santa Rosa in time to complete the mission, so we received a change of mission. My squad had been doing really well—and then, frustration and fatigue crept in. While waiting to receive our new details, everyone just laid down. They didn't even pretend to try; they just curled up on the ground and slept. The change of mission was a double hit to morale since we lost our chow birds AND we would miss Santa Rosa Island, a Ranger School rite of passage. We loaded up in trucks, then we walked.

We hadn't done mission prep for any of this, which resembled how things happen in the real world. The enemy has a say in every fight, so changes in combat are inevitable. None of us had ever looked at this part of the map prior to right now, so getting oriented was extremely difficult. At least the morning PL's and PSG's lack of preparation didn't hurt the new leadership team. We completed our mission and then had a short walk. Land nav on flat land and in a swamp was a lot harder than in the mountains. We did a map check, and I was a full six hundred meters off when pinpointing our location. Fuck. That plus the shit show at the patrol base that morning was enough to fail. Literally, there was no chance of passing this patrol. Fuck! The ambush went well, but my AAR did not.

As if the Ranger gods were speaking directly to me, a storm rolled in as we were walking to the patrol base, adding insult to injury. That night, I did not eat or even open my ruck. I kneeled on the wet ground, leaned my shoulder on my ruck, put my head on my helmet, pulled my poncho over my head, closed my eyes, and laid there lost in my own world of self-pity. A sad and pitiful sight, no doubt.

I'M NOT PASSING,
BUT I'M NOT QUITTING

One of the senior RIs for our company asked if I ever thought about quitting. I definitely did not want to quit. In fact, I can't think of a single time during Florida where I doubted whether or not I belonged. I would never have quit, but I definitely did not want to be there anymore.

I had little to no hope of getting out of Swamps this round, but another squad leader from my last mission said his RI gave him a "Go." Since I knew he screwed up more than me, there was a glimmer of hope. Reengage emotional rollercoaster.

However, on September 13, the cadre confirmed that five of us, including me, were recycling. This one was hard. I couldn't pass Swamps! Only a complete loser recycled Swamps Phase. What was so wrong with me that I couldn't get through this shitty-ass, not-really-that-hard course?

I had to call Allan. He had known before me about each and every "Go" or "No Go" up to this point, so it might be an unnecessary call. I dialed the phone. He picked up. When I heard his voice, I couldn't say anything. I opened my mouth to talk, but nothing came out. I just started crying—actually sobbing. All I could squeak out was, "I ... fucked ... up." A veteran of hard schools himself, he understood and said a few supportive words. I hung up, wiped my face, and returned to the grind.

CHAPTER 11

THE WORST RECYCLE

Swamps Recycle
September 14–25

I was mad and disappointed but didn't feel cheated. It was easy to walk down the road of victimhood at Ranger School, as injustices appeared everywhere I turned. But the problem with victimhood was that it didn't lead anywhere. Being a victim mentally releases people from taking control of their destinies. And I, for one, was going to control this outcome and get my ass to Victory Pond.

Throughout my life, I have been reminded that attitude is the most important part of mental health. I could choose defeat, frustration, and anger, or I could check myself, say a prayer, and continue to revel in the mere fact that after sixty-five years of only allowing men on these hallowed grounds, I was here and able to train with America's best and brightest. I chose the latter.

TROUBLE AT HOME

While I was in Florida waiting to restart Swamps, I got a letter from Allan telling me my dad had cancer, and it was really bad. Like, "He's not coming out of this one," bad. I guess he had had surgery on his neck to remove the cancerous lymph nodes. The surgeon had gone "up" as far as they could but couldn't get it all. I had no idea what any of that meant and was instantly scared shitless. I needed to call Dad—NOW! But I still had to keep my game face on.

We did PT in the morning, ate in the chow hall, and built a sand volleyball court for the Gator Lounge. My body felt like shit, and my brain was spinning. Allan's letter ground at my gut, especially since he hadn't said anything about it when I last called.

After work detail, I talked to the RI on duty and received special permission to make a call. I just couldn't wait any longer. I needed to know before I developed a damn ulcer. First, I called Allan to find out what was going on. He told me everything he knew, explaining he couldn't just throw this huge steaming pile of shit at me on a two-minute call where I could barely communicate through my own misery.

I called Dad next. His speech was slow and slurred. It was so hard to understand him. Allan hadn't explained that the surgery had included removing part of Dad's jawbone and that he had already started radiation on his neck and face. My dad was an extremely handsome man and took pride in his appearance, so this must have been difficult for him. At sixty-nine, he maintained broad shoulders and a tiny waist. Even with fused vertebrae in his back, he stood tall and straight and maintained a soldier's haircut.

I didn't have the relationship I wanted with my dad, but I always tried to make that old soldier proud. I don't really know if I ever did, but this phone call made me realize I might never get the chance. "The first daddy–daughter Ranger graduates" was something I had let myself think about a lot. This Florida recycle might mean he would never see me graduate. My heart broke a lot.

The call was over and so was my opportunity for sulking. There was nothing I could do for my dad. I wrapped up the pity party and got back to my work detail. Of all the things Allan and I talked about, the one thing he had hammered into me before I left for the school was "guard your self-talk." You know that little voice in your head that's you talking to you? When things get hard, that little voice can turn a drizzle into a downpour, and it can also drag you out of a ditch. I controlled that voice. I commanded my downtrodden internal monologue to shut the fuck up because I had three more weeks to go.

MENTAL DEFEAT

It was a nine-week school, and I'd been there five months. I could barely count the days anymore. During this recycle, I was mentally defeated in so many ways, but quitting was further from my mind than ever before. My body felt broken after five months of shit food, crappy fitness, and oscillating sleep patterns, but I planned to finish strong—whatever that looked like. I worked to get myself ready for whatever was coming at me next.

The recycles all had classes. One day, we had a class on the orders process, and I taught it. That helped my confidence while increasing my bitterness. The RI sat in, but all the students asked me questions. Being considered a subject matter expert by my peers and even some of the cadre while still failing tactics was a tough pill to swallow.

I started lying to Allan on the phone. I would tell him that everything was okay. I hated lying to him, but the truth would have been worse on him. My right hip hurt really badly. Running made it so much worse. My right knee and left foot weren't happy either. There was nothing he could do other than stress from eight hundred miles away. I didn't want to verbalize or demonstrate any weaknesses after the crap I dealt with in Darby and Mountains, so I internalized the physical pain with the emotional. The suck was real, but I didn't make it to Florida just to LOM—a despised acronym for quitting from "Lack of Motivation."

Allan told me he loved getting my letters but couldn't sleep after reading them. The letters home to him were time delayed. So, in real time, I failed a phase/got recycled, and then two weeks later, he received a letter saying, "I'm feeling good about my patrols and performance!" Wash, rinse, repeat. It was heartbreaking, I'm sure. Although I was sending the letters to my family, I was really writing for my own mental fitness. I needed an outlet for my emotions. I needed to feel like I was sharing this experience with the people most important to me. I needed to feel like I wasn't a thirty-seven-year-old, female island stranded in a sea of young, male soldiers who hated me. I needed to write, and I needed to know that someone was reading those letters and empathizing. When Allan told me he couldn't read my letters, he inadvertently stole my only outlet. He was my rock but was suffering as much as I was with all the demands on him. I couldn't express to him how truly hurt I was.

But the real kicker came when I picked up my last FedEx box. I received articles questioning the validity of female graduates from Ranger School. Congressman Steve Russell, a Republican from Oklahoma and himself a graduate of Ranger School, was demanding documentation proving Shaye Haver and Kristen Griest had really passed. With that, I went from kind of nervous to scared shitless. I prayed the RIs didn't grade me even harder out of fear of repercussions due to all this bullshit media coverage. No one wanted to be the RI that graduated the thirty-seven-year-old, mother-of-two reservist as it was. The "what if"s kept popping into my mind. I tried pushing them down and maintaining my focus. It was really hard.

I just wished I understood what it was about last cycle that didn't click with me. This stuff was easy, and I understood it. I could answer any question and tell you when anybody else messed up. I still thought my PSG mission should have been a "Go." My RI said my team leaders were to blame for my squad leader failure. And my first look as a PL was good, except there was fratricide that no one knew about—and the squad leaders who committed that fratricide all graduated last week. All my patrols were so close to passing. Any one of them could have been a "Go" with one slight change. That was the thing: even after all this time, I didn't know how to defend against the subjectivity in grading. And after five months of inconsistent grading and higher-than-normal standards, this politician had the balls to say we received unfair advantages. How about unfair disadvantages? That guy ensured I would have to be perfect to pass. Not close. Not good. Perfect. Perfect was subjective. And even if I was perfect while in charge, if the other students in leadership positions didn't support my perfection campaign, I was sunk.

Please, God, let me smash this one out of the ballpark.

CHAPTER 12

"LET'S DO IT FOR LISA"

Swamps 2

September 26–October 16

I really did not want to restart this shit. I had to bond with another group of men, building fresh relationships with guys that didn't really want any new friends. It felt forced, not natural. I was so ready to be done with all this nonsense. Proving myself daily for almost six months was fucking exhausting. I just wanted to go. Go anywhere. Go home. Go to the moon. Just go away from this place.

But if I was going to get through Swamps, I had to start my next round on the right foot. When the new guys got off the bus, I addressed them immediately. I found out who was their leader and gave him the lowdown on the recycles, what the rest of the day looked like, how we prepped the company area and their gear before they arrived, and that we needed them to check that nothing was missing first and foremost. Their PL immediately acknowledged he could see I was going to be a useful resource, and I recognized that his platoon had been successful together for a while and assured him that we, as recycles, just wanted to fit in and help.

Then I addressed the elephant in the room for all to hear. "Yes. I am in fact a woman. Yes. I am still here. Yes. I have been here for a long fucking time. No. I don't need special care or assistance. And yes. We are all staying in the same barracks."

That seemed to get everyone to stop gawking at me like I had a horn growing out of my forehead. There were a few nervous giggles, a couple knowing nods, a respectful hand gesture or two, and, finally, a look of disdain from at least one "nonbeliever."

LAST MARKETING CAMPAIGN

This platoon was good and much more cohesive than the last. I needed to push really hard to Peer well since I felt lazy every morning and my stomach was constantly upset. Plus, they were already a close-knit group before making it to Swamps. I had to become indispensable. I worried because C-1, our squad, had a 100 percent "Go" rate last cycle. That meant they definitely would not allow nine for nine this round. No one wanted to get the reputation of being the "easy" RI.

I was assigned to be the M240 gunner for the training exercises on our first day running around with this new class. Mark that up to one more statistical anomaly. We also switched to winter gear, which meant my ruck was bursting at the seams. The heavier ruck plus being the M240 gunner drained my soul! I felt unfit and stagnant. But I knew if I kept going, I would get used to it in a few days.

My morale was low, and Allan not wanting me to write him anymore took away my only pressure release. I couldn't complain to these guys and let them see any weakness. I felt like I was talking to my best friend when I was writing. I could still write, but knowing Allan wasn't going to read it decreased the therapeutic effect and fractured my resilience. I remember watching an episode of *Desperate Housewives* where one of the wives had cancer, and her husband explained that although she had the affliction, he also dealt with emotional pain. I guess that's what Allan went through. My bad days were worse for him because he could not help or take away my hardship.

One evening, as soon as we got back to the barracks, a couple guys jumped right into the shower, even though this platoon had decided the most efficient way for everyone to use the shower was for me to get in and out first. I took three minutes from clothes on to clothes on and not a second more. Once I finished, the guys had free reign for the rest of the night. These guys jumping to the front of the shower line was no big deal for me. I would just get ready for tomorrow and, if necessary, go to sleep nasty and shower after everyone else went to bed, as I was accustomed to from prior platoons. At this point, I didn't give a damn. Well, some of my new teammates got pissed—like, fisticuffs pissed—at their peers. I didn't need this drama. The pissed-off group of guys cleared the showers for me. I took the fastest shower ever. Then I laid out all my wet gear and headed straight to bed. It was 2300.

I got up at 0400 the next morning to pack my ruck. Of course, there was nobody up for fire guard, so I woke the assigned guards and went back to bed at 0430 once I was packed and ready for the day. The real reason I woke up the guards was because I knew the guy assigned to that time was planning to pack and would be in a world of hurt when it was time to step off if I didn't wake him. I made sure to set my alarm for 0500 to wake the remaining guys.

Back to mothering a new group of boys, I guess. I wondered if the oldest or most senior in each group usually took on this role?

I wish I knew why I couldn't seem to pass this damn course. I had two guys tell me they could not believe I recycled. They said I was too squared away to still be here. One SF guy said that when people asked him tactical questions, he just sent them over to me. "Ask Jaster—she knows this shit better than anybody here."

On our second day in the field, we had a long walk that was interrupted by OP4. Everyone was dragging ass and reacted slowly, so the RIs made it into a mass-casualty event. I wasn't in any type of leadership position, but as usual, I felt the need to help out. People were so busy worrying about individuals that no one was creating a proper triage-and-treatment area. I got everything set up and handed the reins back to the assigned leadership. The RI asked me why I had taken over. I told him I was not as familiar with medical treatment methods as many of these enlisted soldiers, but

I am fully trained at organization and keeping people calm during stress events. That seemed to be good enough for him.

When we started walking again, one of the Ranger students on his second or third attempt at this school brought up my actions with regard to taking care of the injured soldiers. He told the day's leadership that if they got a "Go," it was because I got it for them. The RIs were testing us with that event. It wasn't planned, which indicated they were on the fence as to whether that day's leadership could properly execute a Ranger mission.

At that point, I had invested enough in each of these guys to where they accepted me as a teammate. They figured out that getting up, running around, organizing the casualties, and doing extra work when I could have just been lying on the ground was normal Jaster behavior. They'd either get their tab with me in a few weeks or have a story to tell about how they were with me when I failed Swamps for the second time and washed out of the school after six months.

During this round of Swamps, we actually executed the Santa Rosa Island mission. I guess I would be able to call myself a "real Ranger" after all. We did not get the helo insert, but we did get a short bus ride—nap time!

For once, during the Santa Rosa Island mission, I had no real job. I carried some extra squad equipment, but I was not in leadership, nor did I have a big gun. We got off the bus at the beachhead and loaded rubber boats for the trip out to the island. I did some great compass work as a boat captain and tried to get those tired thugs to row straight. Noise and light disciplines were difficult when you had a squad of exhausted twenty-somethings trying to kill the water with paddles. My Ranger School path seemed to be to lead from within, even when I wasn't getting graded on my leadership. I guess that was why these guys accidentally called me Mama Ranger at times, and I protected them like they were my kin. Even the RIs gave up pulling me out of positions of influence. At least, that's what I thought.

When we got to the island and set up in our positions, I was excited to assault the objective, and the RI heard me reminding the squad leader of a few things he'd forgotten. I was desperate to get everyone their "Go." If I didn't pass patrols at this Godforsaken school, I was going to at least leave with everyone else saying that I helped them with tactics and was an amazing team member. The RI decided to fix my little red wagon and "shot" me, taking me out of the action.

Shy of getting a "Go," getting shot was the absolute pinnacle of the course. My job was to fall to the ground, and I chose to also wail with anguish. After all my frustrations, I took off my "major" veneer and acted *exactly* how I felt. I wailed and hollered and thrashed around on the ground, acting my injury to the best of my ability. The RI quickly returned and "killed" me, saying it was a little too real and he didn't want to hear that shit.

If I thought it was hard to stay awake in the prone while waiting for the signal to initiate an attack or ambush, staying awake while lying motionless on my back on the beach was impossible. So I drifted off to a restful slumber in the middle of a full-on firefight with blanks. The mission ended, and the platoon swept through the site and completed their actions on the objective. When completing the casualty-collection portion of the mission, no one could find me at first. Luckily, the surviving members of my squad paused and shushed everybody to listen for my distinct snore. Shockingly, I was then easy to find. We completed our mission, I was resurrected, and we headed back on the rubber boats, giggling and telling stories of mock combat. Even the RI got in on the bullshitting, saying that was one Santa Rosa mission he would never forget.

A couple guys offered a squad mantra of "Let's do it for Lisa." It wasn't a "Remember the Alamo"-type rallying call, but it was enough to make me feel like maybe at least a very thin slice of the Army was in fact ready for integration; at least a few stinky, tired, young alpha males were.

JUST ONE OF THE GUYS

As a member of Gen X, I hear a vast assortment of complaints about the younger generations, especially millennials. The business world is still trying to figure out how they fit, and the Army keeps adjusting how it adapts to the rapidly changing culture. One of my biggest takeaways from living with these young bucks for six months is they are a lot more open-minded and willing to go with the flow than any previous generation. I think most of them accepted me as part of the team before even I was ready to be a "bro."

Even on my worst days, I faked motivation, but one particular day was especially long, and my shoulder ached. It was pitch black and chilly. Everyone was leaning against their rucks since we had just completed our AAR. I looked around and decided to plop down on my ruck just like everyone else. Seeing my "ruck flop" after everyone else's must have been the straw that broke the cool, southern demeanor of one of the other Ranger students. He flew over to me, yelling at me to get off my ass and get ready for movement. He was always a gentle soul with a Georgia drawl, so it shocked some motivation into my legs.

I thought, "Hell. Lee's never upset. I musta' really fucked up." I sat up quick and tried to stand my ass up. The getting down had been easy—getting up, not so much. You had two options for standing up with an eighty-plus-pound ruck on your back. You could roll over and try to get on your hands and knees, ultimately crawling to a standing position, or you could grab a buddy's hands while he stepped on your feet and yanked you up with a jerk. The idea of rolling over and getting to my feet had zero appeal. Since Lee was standing right at my feet, livid, I thought we'd just put some of that rage to good use. "Help me up!" I said.

When I reached my hands out, "asking" Lee for a boost, he immediately went from furious to friendly. "Oh, damn, Jaster. I'm sorry. I thought you were one of the guys." He was a young LT raised to respect both women and his elders. I was both to him.

Once he helped me up, the pissed-off tables turned. I was pissed, and he was in receive mode from a major. I lit his ass up with some on-the-spot professional development about not letting my adjectives sway him from upholding the standard. It was one-way and heated at first, but once I had his attention, I moved it to a conversational tone, and we had a constructive chat. And once again, I realized why I really needed to be at Ranger School.

Not everyone took quite as long as Lee to see me as one of the guys. A couple of them even got TOO comfortable with me.

We were probably on our fourth or fifth day of the FTX when the temperature dropped significantly. After we crossed the river and trudged through the swamp, the RIs started worrying as we all shivered. We didn't have a lot of fat on us anymore. We stopped at the far side of the swamp and changed into slightly less wet uniforms.

I walked a few feet away behind some shrubs and changed. If somebody really tried hard, they could have seen some white ass with heat rash, but nothing exciting. I left my boots off as long as possible, just walking around barefoot to avoid losing anymore skin from my pinky toes or my last two remaining toenails.

All of a sudden, I heard one of my buddies yelling my name. He seemed really excited about something. I hurried in his direction with my ruck in one hand and my boots in the other. When I got there, he couldn't stop yammering at me. He was talking so fast I couldn't get a word in edgewise.

When he finally took a breath, I just blurted out, "Dude, you're naked."

He simply replied, "Yeah, so?" And then he continued his story, standing there in his birthday suit. By the time he finished his story, the entire platoon was staring at him.

I just snickered, turned around, and walked away.

I heard some muffled giggles and a few snorts, and then he yelled, "Shit, Jaster. My bad. I forgot you were a girl."

As I returned to the little wooded patch that was my dressing room, I felt a little tightness in my throat. OMG. I was choked up! It seems ridiculous now, but that was the biggest compliment I could have received. I would never again let myself be concerned about women ruining the "mystical bro-bond" required for effective combat operations.

PROTECTIVE DETAIL

On October 6, I was point man again. I loved leading the platoon through the woods from the front, but it was exhausting. Of course, I was still trying to do as much as possible to make sure everyone knew I was a team player. But when the RI saw me heading out to lead the formation again, he stopped the platoon. "Nope. Not you, Jaster. Somebody else take point."

After we had walked a significant distance, the RI got nervous about our plan. He started asking individuals in the formation, starting at the back, if anyone knew where we were. It was difficult to track our location because everything was flat in that part of Florida, and there were few identifiers to help orient yourself to the map.

When the RI got to me, I easily pointed to within fifty meters of our actual position. The RI snorted and said, "Goddamn, Jaster. How do you do that? Do you have an illegal GPS on your watch?"

I knew he was joking, but the guys were defensive of me. They knew my story well enough from the newspapers they read before even reporting to Ranger School, but the image of a woman with lower standards didn't mesh with reality. I worked hard to endear myself to each soldier by helping them out when they were in leadership positions. They saw me teach classes, take care of others, share my food, write orders for others, and even carry extra shit. After working with me the past week, they couldn't figure out why I was still there.

Hearing the RI joke about me cheating struck a nerve in the class leader, as the person responsible for admin actions and organizing the students. He walked around the squad saying, "If Lisa's getting fucked with this bad now, imagine the first five months she was here. We will get her a 'Go.' Now it's our job, not hers."

Sometimes units find cohesion around injustices. Real or perceived injustices create a chip on the collective shoulder. I became Class 10-15's chip. It became us against the RIs to get me a "Go." What started as my worst phase of Ranger School turned into my best experience yet. These were my guys. This was my team.

LAST HURRAH!

By the end of our time in the field, I had either lost all of my pens, or they had been "borrowed" and not returned. All I had left were colored pens and map markers. Apparently, the RIs were now looking over the PL's and point man's shoulders during FRAGO briefings to make sure they didn't see anything written in colored pen. So, when I did what I had done for months, which was write OPORDs for these junior soldiers who had absolutely no clue how to write one, the RI knew I helped. I was informed I was no longer allowed to help the guys write their orders or plan their mission routes unless I was in an assigned leadership position.

No fucking way was I going to stop helping. If I was in the lead squad, I *always* made the route. And if I wasn't, I sat on the line at my fighting position along the patrol base perimeter and wrote the execution plan. I knew the guys wanted my help because they kept bringing me black pens. There were plenty of competent officers and NCOs who were extremely successful and didn't NEED me, but writing orders was second nature for a field-grade officer, and I wanted to allow these young soldiers to focus on all the other things they were responsible for while being graded. This potentially built cohesion between the ranks, which is something the Army desperately needs. Too often, there is a divide between officers and enlisted, especially in environments like this. I frequently hear enlisted folks say things like, "Don't call me 'sir.' I work for a living." If that line doesn't express a ton of issues between the ranks, I don't know what does.

There was a selfish reason I helped, too. Staying engaged made the time go by much faster and kept me from droning during movements. And at this point, it also made everyone in Swamps endeared to me. These young, cocky little assholes wouldn't admit to much, but they frequently told me I saved their asses. Because I wanted to keep that trend going, disobeying the RIs about helping out saved my ass as well.

The last day of patrolling at Ranger School started as poorly as every other day. I was not going to get another graded patrol. We received the mission, and I wasn't assigned a position. Hopefully, that meant I was a "Go," but at this point, I'd proved to be a terrible prognosticator, so I didn't bother speculating my future.

I knew the last walk of the day was right around the corner. It was a real bitch, and no one would be highly motivated for it. As usual, I helped with the mission-planning effort and did everything I could to try to keep the team moving in the right direction. The patrol base had what looked like an old, wooden hunting-ground blind on it. We wrote our order in there, which allowed for a lot more freedom of movement than we usually had. The blind was not in the center of the patrol base, so I could easily hide that I was helping from the RIs. The assigned leadership was extremely junior, and they had little to no experience with mission planning, writing orders, and briefing. It was funny. I camped in my little blind, and the PL, PSG, and a couple of the squad leaders bopped back and forth to come chat with me. This was my jam, and, tab or not, I was going to end on a good note.

The FRAGO briefing was complete. I couldn't hear anything, but I knew it was over when we were told to start movement. We went straight to the road, which was a little odd. Nothing happened to us as we moved from the patrol base to the release point, but then the RIs told us there was a change in plans. We all took a knee, facing out along either side of the road. Then we were told to "just relax." We all sat on our rucks and glanced around, trying to figure out what the hell was going on.

Ten minutes, which felt like thirty, later, the RI switched me to squad leader, and then we got moving. No prep. No discussion. No change-over brief. Nothing. Had I not helped write the OPORD and been intimately familiar with the mission for the day already, I would have been royally fucked. Had I not disobeyed the RI's directive to disengage from planning, I would have had zero chance of doing anything other than wrecking this patrol. Not only would I have failed, most likely, I would have been so bad that everybody else in the leadership would have failed as well.

The abrupt switch definitely didn't go unnoticed. The platoon got red in the face en masse. Every last dude in C-Co of Class 10-15 was pissed, even the ones who didn't want a female soldier at Ranger School with them. The whispers started immediately, and "Do it for Lisa" was mumbled by all. In that moment, I knew I may never graduate Ranger School, but I wouldn't fail that patrol because of teamwork issues.

My last patrol at Ranger School is seared into my memory. We were in a big, open field, and Clap and I were in position at the edge of the woods. Where I was on my seventh phase of Ranger School, Clap was on his sixth. By this time, we were close, and it was good to be with him on the last mission of the last day. The actual ambush was set up beautifully. We waited for the signal to initiate. I could not imagine a better Ranger School mission execution. I was happy. All that was left to my Ranger School experience was to fire my weapon, transition to the AAR, and start the long walk back to the airfield and barracks. I was going home by the end of the week. Clap too. We were giddy. I had some drink mix hidden in my pocket for a little "celebration" in our fighting position.

We stayed in the prone, but our minds were already at Victory Pond. Then one of the RIs started walking the line. *WTF is this guy doing? The RIs never walk out in front of the positions, especially on an ambush.* I crouch-walked to the first position just after the RI strolled past. As he gently meandered past the position, I noticed he had a weapon in his far-side hand. He wasn't acting as an RI; he was acting as a recon element for the OP4. "Oh shit!"

I clicked my weapon off safe and dumped a magazine in him, waking up the asshole sitting in the position I just came upon. Fuck! The guy I was moving to check on, my guy, was fast asleep and completely missed the enemy. The RI was being sneaky. If he noticed my guy sleeping, I failed. The soldier in that position, another recycle buddy of mine, teared up when he realized I was a "No Go" because he was sleeping. This is my luck.

As crushed as I was, I wasn't going to let this ruin my last day in the field at Ranger School. On the bright side, my shots initiated the ambush. There I was, emptying my magazines and assaulting through the objective while trying to make my Ranger buddy feel better. It wasn't his fault. The dude was exhausted, and I had had plenty of opportunities to pass. Just like in a football game. It's not the kicker who missed the extra point's fault that his team lost the game. That kick was merely one of many missed opportunities. By the time we sat down for the AAR, he felt better, but I felt worse.

As we walked back, the RI pulled me to the side to give me a walking AAR. This particular RI had previously won the "Best Ranger" competition two times and was an absolute legend among the Ranger battalions. As I walked beside him, time slowed down, and the gravity of the next few minutes of chit chat between me and this RI was not lost on me. This was *it*.

For positives, he told me I had solid initiative and gave good recommendations to my team leads. He was impressed with both my communications and teamwork. He only gave me two negatives, but they were big ones. The first negative was "comprehensive fitness." With these words, I had to restrain a slight smirk. "Comprehensive fitness" was basically a dig at your physical state. He called me "weak." But there was a twist to this. IF an RI gave you "comprehensive fitness" as a *positive* from your patrol event, it meant with utmost certainty you failed and did not get a "Go." But I got it as a negative. I wasn't sure what to make of "comprehensive fitness" as a negative, but I had an idea that my RI just gave me a verbal "atta girl." But I had thought I was good before, so I decided not to read into it. The next negative was "tactical and technical competence." Ouch, that one hurt. He pointed out several things tactically that were incorrect with my ambush and dismissed me curtly to return to my spot in the formation.

"What did he say?" a buddy asked.

"Um, yeah. That two-time Ranger of the Year awardee just told me I was not physically fit, and I don't understand tactics. That's a pretty solid indicator I am going home without my tab." How else could I reasonably interpret my counseling? There was just no way I could twist that conversation into a "Go."

I fell back into my spot for the remainder of the movement. The guys were having a terrible time keeping their spacing and moving tactically. They were done with Ranger School and didn't care about this final movement. They were right not to care anymore. The votes were in. But here I was, still in a graded billet until relieved.

Still hoping that a good final movement might add that extra sway to allow me to get a "Go" and get the fuck out of Swamps. Who was I kidding? This shit was over.

October 10 turned into October 11. Around 0100, we were all on our gear, waiting. The cadre members approached our useless, smelly gaggle, and 1SG yelled, "Jaster!" I headed over for my final course counseling. I dropped my gear and shuffled over to him. I stood at parade rest. "Yes, First Sergeant."

His comments were short and pointed. It was done. After six months, it was finally over. I was a motherfucking "Go" for graduation. I was headed to Victory Pond.

Somehow my squad knew before I did. Figures. When I turned around from my counseling, they were bouncing around like a kindergarten class after a birthday party. I didn't realize until I saw their faces that each member of my squad felt my success was their success as well. I was their sister in arms, but I struggled to find happiness in that moment. The guys could not have been more supportive and happy for me, while I stood there in frustrated elation. I had accomplished my goal—not my original goal of being one of the first or proving to the world that women could hold their own in an austere environment when a lot is on the line. I accomplished my other goal, the one that came when I was sent back to Day One of RAP week. I truly changed the hearts and minds of future leaders in the US Army. But now what? How do I deal with the aftermath of doubt and the bullshit associated with taking six months to complete a nine-week school? How many excellent soldiers were graded harder or didn't pass because they were assigned leadership positions with me, getting stuck under my microscope? How many soldiers were ostracized or challenged because they decided to treat me as an equal at this school? What now?

Later on, prior to leaving Florida, the BC called me to the side to chat and told me it easily could have gone either way. He could have passed or failed me. No matter what he chose, a lot of people were going to question him and hate him. I thought him saying that was poor form.

His comments hung in my mind, and they bothered me. Why was there any doubt when the guys I shared foxholes with cried when they thought I wasn't going to graduate, and then cried again when they found out I would? Tell me how having the utmost support from a platoon of alpha males who ate and slept next to me in the field for ten days wasn't enough proof I belonged and deserved to graduate.

*LtCol Allan Jaster pinning my Ranger Tab on
my shoulder with my kids and mom.*

*Members of my United States Military Academy
graduating class presenting me a signed banner.*

Standing in my final formation at Ranger School waiting to be released to my family and friends waiting in the bleachers.

CONCLUSION

CLOSE OUT

There's a challenge with being a "first" when you really just want to be accepted. When I applied to Ranger School, I wasn't setting out to enter the public eye. I just wanted to be the best engineer, the best officer, and the best soldier I could be.

The reason I have a public platform and a voice is the exact thing I fought so hard against. I am a reserve officer in the United States Army. I have done project management and construction management for over twenty years in one capacity or another. I am a parent. I am an athlete. I take pride in being all those things, but I want to be great at each and every one. I don't want to be good for a woman. I am a woman, but as an officer or manager, I want to be the best—not the best woman in the running, just the best, or at least the best that I can possibly be. Is it important to have firsts and break glass ceilings? YUP! But then, we need to look at merit and not race, gender, creed, or any other adjective. I have a platform because I am an OLD, FEMALE soldier who passed

Ranger School—but I want to use that platform to make the best voices heard based on merit.

After graduation, I had the opportunity to attend then-President Barack Obama's last State of the Union address. While waiting for the event to start, I was called into a side room, where I met every military senior leader, including the Joint Chiefs of Staff. When I asked General Mark Milley, then Chief of Staff of the Army, what I could do for the Army after being given such a fantastic opportunity, his answer was simple. "Come back into the active Army, branch transfer to infantry, and lead from the front during this time of change."

My answer was equally as simple, "Hell, no, sir. I love the engineers. I have spent all my time trying to be an amazing engineer. What is option two, sir?"

You should have seen the expression on his aide's face when I said "no" to the highest-ranking man in the entire US Army. Priceless.

General Milley then followed up with, "Be visible, MAJ Jaster. People need to see you and your success."

I didn't completely understand why that was important back then, and at the time, I really wasn't interested in advertising my six months in a two-month school. But recently, I heard the statement, "You cannot be what you cannot see." That has never been the case for me, so I couldn't comprehend letting the successes or failures of others dictate my desire to try something new.

A lot has changed over the past seven years, but most of it has been adding maturity and empathy to my preexisting positions. I have been blessed with a stage to share my message since graduating in October 2015 and met a plethora of people who are NOTHING like me but are interested in my story. For them, seeing an old lady with kids succeed where others have failed was the motivation they needed to quit their old job and start a new career, say "yes" to the man of their dreams, or start eating a bit healthier every day. They just needed to see someone they could relate to overcome an obstacle, any obstacle.

Sharing my story, as General Milley requested, doesn't just impact others. It has a lasting influence on what paths I personally choose.

Being public about my personal trials, tribulations, and successes forces me to live outside my comfort zone. I am judged harshly and regularly. I am glad that I am. I am getting older, slower, uglier, whatever—and better. I read more. I empathize more. I push myself harder and am finally willing to share my lowlights along with my highlights. I don't know what the world holds next for me, but I know I am not done.

In the meantime, I hope my little story motivates at least one person to say, "Fuck it," and go all in. If I could shave my head for this shit, what are you willing to do to reach your goals?

GLOSSARY

1SG: First Sergeant

A-Co/B-Co/C-Co: A-Company/B-Company/C-Company

AAR: After Action Review

Actions on the objective: Series of combat activities starting with preparing the area of interest, executing the designated mission, and ending with transitioning to the next mission.

ACU: Army Combat Uniforms

Arty: artillery simulators

AT4: A weapon that fires an 84 mm high-explosive anti-tank warhead through a tube

ATL/BTL: Alpha Team Leader, Bravo Team Leader

AXP: Ambulance Exchange Points

Azimuth: Direction the team needs to travel, usually guided by a compass reading

Black-and-gold plan: Withdrawal routes should we get overrun

Boards: Process for reviewing the performance of a soldier and deciding the next steps for the individual.

Bolo: military slang for "failed"

Branching armor: "Branching" is the process of receiving a field career assignment, sometimes based on military requirement (force branched), but usually by choice. "Armor" is a branch of the Army that is combat arms and focuses on tanks. It is responsible for tank and cavalry/forward reconnaissance operations on the battlefield.

Break contact: When one force engaged in combat choses to pull out of the military engagement, moving away to a safe distance.

BUD/S: Navy SEAL training

Calling the bird: Making radio contact with the helicopter.

CASEVAC: casualty evacuation

CCP: Casualty Collection Points

CWSA: Combat Water Survival Assessment

DFAC: military dining facility (a.k.a. chow hall)

DZ: Drop Zone

EXFIL: exfiltration (or extraction)

FLA: Field Litter Ambulance

FLC: Fighting Load Carrier

FM: Field Manual

FO: forward observer

FRAGO: Fragmentary Order

FTX: Field Training Exercise

FUD: Female Urinary Device

HMMWV: High Mobility Multipurpose Wheeled Vehicle

Hooch: A makeshift place to live/sleep, usually temporary.

HVT: High Value Target

In the prone: Laying as flat as possible on the stomach with weapon oriented toward the enemy

IN: Infantry

INFIL: infiltration

Land Navigation: Locating a point on the ground using a US Army Military Grid, map, and usually a compass.

LDA: Linear Danger Area

LOM: lack of motivation

LZ: landing zone

Major Minus: A tracked negative credit given to Ranger School students for failing to complete a task or activity to standard.

Major Plus: A tracked positive credit given to Ranger School students for excelling in a specific area.

MEDEVAC: Medical Evacuation

MRE: Meal Ready to Eat

NCO: non-commissioned officers

ND: To accidentally shoot your weapon

NVG: night-vision goggles

OA: Observer/Advisor program. Female company grade officers and non-commissioned officers who volunteered to work in the field at Ranger School to ensure a safe and effective integration process.

OP4: Opposition Forces

OPORD: Operations Order

ORP: Objective rally point that is out of sight, sound, and small-arms range of the objective area; where the unit stages prior to an attack to complete final preparations and potentially return to after the completion of the mission.

ORSA: Operations Research/Systems Analysis

Pace count: Specific number of steps an individual takes to cover a designated distance usually 100 meters. This will vary depending on the person, terrain, injury (taking shorter steps), running vs. walking, and load being carried.

PE: Practical Exercise

PL: platoon leader

PLF: Parachute Landing Fall

PSG: platoon sergeant

PT: physical training

Pulled the slip: Pulling the risers that lead from the soldier to the canopy of their parachute in order to manipulate their flight pattern.

RAP: Ranger Assessment Phase

Recon: reconnaissance

Reveille: wake up

RI: Ranger Instructor

RPFT: Ranger Physical Fitness Test

RTAC: Ranger Training Assessment Course

RTB: Ranger Training Battalion

RTO: Radio Telephone Operator

RTT: Ranger Training Tasks

SAW: Squad Automatic Weapon

SFC: Sergeant First Class

Sham: To pretend to push while really taking it easy

SkedCo: Plastic sheet used as a litter to carry casualties

SL: squad leaders

SNAFU: Situation Normal: All Fucked Up

Snivel gear: Gear meant to protect you from the elements

SOR: Serious Observation Reports

TLP: Troop Leading Procedures

TMC: the médical clinic

TRADOC: Training Command

WARNO: Warning Order